The Bar Shift

By Dave Nitzel and Dave Domzalski

www.thebarshift.com

Table of Contents

Process and Service

Financials

*To our beautiful families
for all their love, support, and encouragement.*

Foreword

By Sean Finter

"You wanna know the secret to ending up with a million bucks in the bar business? Start with two million, kid!"

A neighboring restaurant owner barked that gem of advice from across the street. It was the night of the soft opening of my first restaurant in Sydney, Australia. I was 27 and hadn't slept for weeks. I landed in Australia two years earlier with my backpack, a Canadian passport, $7,300 and a willingness to swing for the fences. I had entered an industry where the majority of those before failed. The rollercoaster of bar/restaurant ownership was just beginning.

Nothing can fully prepare you for running bars and restaurants. It demands more than you have physically each shift. But it's the emotional toll that knocks so many out of the game. When a hardware store goes bankrupt people are quick to point out that you can't compete with the big box stores. When a bar or restaurant closes, someone's dream dies. Not to mention that Thanksgiving and Christmas take on a new level of awkward with "The 3 F's", the Family, Friends and Fools that backed that dream financially.

What gave me the confidence to pursue leadership in hospitality was this simple advice that I wrote on the cover of my daily journal "Be brilliant at the basics and everything else will work itself out." This book will help you do just that. You NEED to be brilliant at the basics and it is harder than it sounds.

If you are reading this, it means you see room for improvement. I encourage you not to only discover the potential of your business, but your own self as well, and every single person who works for you. I encourage you to not simply seek to be better, but to find out what the best version of yourself looks like. Then challenge each team member you have, to do the same. Every person that works for you will leave BETTER or BITTER. Better staff = engaged guests.

In my transition from management to ownership over the course of 5 years, I had bootstrapped a group of bars and restaurants that employed hundreds of people and generated tens of millions in revenue using principles just like the ones in the pages that follow. Out of the blue, I received an offer on my business and I knew I was ready for my next challenge. I sold my portfolio and then launched my next business, Barmetrix.

Some say I got lucky in the hospitality business. I disagree. It wasn't luck, it wasn't because I was smarter than my competition and it wasn't because I worked harder. There is a formula to business much like there is to health. The right combination of calories, sleep and exercise. The formula for the hospitality business is slightly more complicated but you will find it within this book.

I learned firsthand that running bars is a very tough way to earn a living. The pace is frantic, countless things can and do go wrong during any given shift, staff are transient, and guests are fickle. This and more takes a toll on management and ownership.

It's a crazy business model. You are opening a business where everyone will have to work opposite hours to their friends and families. You'll pay most of them minimum wage and hope the customers make up the difference for some with tips. And to make it more interesting, you'll crank up the music, turn down the lights and sell liquid drugs!

Most people reading this book are running "for profit" companies. If you are a manager or an owner, you have an obligation to make your organization money. If you have ever worked for a company on the razor's edge, you will know that most people who work there reflect that. Worse still, if you have worked for a bar/restaurant that is losing money every month, you know the desperation and anxiety that spreads through every member of the team.

Many of my early mentors shared their wisdom with me through books. I didn't just read those books, I used them as a tool to build and shape my business. I used to tell my team that there were no original problems in business. We chose to learn from those that came before us. I dog-eared the pages, highlighted passages of relevance and brought those books into team meetings. I suggest you do the same with this one.

I was honored to be asked to write the foreword to this book. Our industry needs more generous teachers willing to share their wisdom. Dave and Dave are two of the most genuine and generous people I know. Together they have decades of experience and I'm thrilled that they decided to share it with all of us. It makes sense that they become mentors. They both get more joy from helping others than they do their own success. The advice you read comes from years in the trenches of personal leadership experience and from coaching hundreds of bar/restaurant operators like you.

My hope is that this book is just the start for Dave, Dave, me and you; that this book becomes a hub for continued education, collaboration and celebration.

Onwards and upwards,

Sean

Preface

When we set out to write a book, we really wanted to target best practices that are both simple and repeatable as well as being key success drivers in your business. We hope you find that we've put an emphasis on breaking down the opportunities into easy to understand chapters targeting some of the top needs of a Bar Manager.

We were very intentional about delivering content that will help Bar Managers both personally and professionally. We believe the amazing people in our industry deserve a high-quality work life that translates to high-quality personal life: ultimately that is our mission! Our chapters are born of proven global best practices from within our industry combined with best practices from large corporate organizations outside our industry that when properly applied can make a massive impact on your personal and professional well-being.

The big idea is to simplify this business in such a way that turns the tables on our typical success rates. The idea of a 40-70% failure rate in our industry is simply unacceptable and unnecessary. So often the line between success and failure in our industry is such a very slim one, just one of these chapters could very well be that one thing that turns your fortunes.

Fortunately, we don't just have one chapter, we wrote Forty-One! It's also important to note, we certainly could have written more and on a variety of different topics. We went through a process of selecting chapters based on things we felt were either most impactful, received very little attention, or were less commonly discussed. Perhaps there's a volume two in the future...but let's not get ahead of ourselves right?

In our day to day business we get to work with some of the most successful Bar and Restaurant Operators all around the world. We not only work with venues on a daily basis, but we're also involved in global leadership coaching; which allows us unprecedented access to what some of the best and brightest are doing, as well as some of the most significant challenges faced in the industry. This was the impetus for writing a book: Dave and I thought we had a real chance to broadcast success in a series of simple and executable best practices in a way that would drive financial and emotional well-being in our industry. Dave and I together then decided we wanted to target the Bar Manager as our core audience for a number of reasons.

Primarily, there's very little content out there specific to Bar Managers and Bar Management. Yes, there's a lot of cocktail books and there's a lot of books about opening and owning a bar but we were looking for something slightly different. So, our focus became if we can help the key position that's responsible for the primary profit center wouldn't that provide maximum lift for everyone involved? That's how The Bar Shift came to life. We also understand that a number of people can play the role of a Bar Manager; it could be anyone from an owner to a Bartender and anyone in between. So even if there's not an official "Bar Manager," all the content applies to anyone serving in the role.

Briefly, a little about us: my career in management began in 1989 and 2019 will mark thirty years of pure managerial bliss. My first 25 years in leadership roles came inside the corporate structure of Fortune 500 companies like UPS, Office Depot and Advance Auto Parts, massive organizations with prolific training programs and resources to ensure there are processes and systems in place that allow for those who are the best and most inspired managers the ability to grow and develop within their respective organizations.

What I've learned in my time in hospitality is that those types of resources rarely exist in our world and those that do are largely proprietary.

I made a very adventurous move into the world of consulting with a specific focus on the hospitality industry. I started a small consulting group with my son Alex; someone had to do the hard work, along with our friend John Huckeba, an industry pro with 30 plus years industry experience, and off we went as the newly minted Rally5 Consultants. At first our work started largely on the inventory management side of things which is rewarding and continues to flourish. We had years of inventory knowledge from working in retail and supply chain solutions, but we really needed some sophistication to complement the guiding principles that we believed to be true. So, after much research and deliberation we purchased a few Barmetrix franchises because we really identified with their core mission which was centered around the simple idea of helping people improve professionally and personally which was a perfect match!

It was in my on-going journey with Barmetrix that I met David Domzalski, a former operator, the corporate trainer at Barmetrix, and who has recently taken on the work of becoming a thought leader and consultant in the Miami market. I consider David a valued friend and advisor whom I turn to on a regular basis for guidance on all things hospitality. Overall, I really wanted, and needed, his experience and expertise to ensure we had-hard core honest content that a Bar Manager could rely upon as well as ensuring our content thoroughly hit the mark.

Thankfully, David enthusiastically agreed to take this journey with me and off we went writing our book!

Here's how we hope you use the book. Firstly, each lesson stands on its own, so you don't have to read it stem to stern to get the full benefit. We thought this was a good idea for our industry. Ideally all the lessons are read and applied as needed, of course. We also hope you share the book with bartenders and aspiring managers with the idea of developing your team and making life easier on yourself through shared learning. So, as I mentioned, we worked hard to come up with a series of practical lessons that could be simply understood and easily applied. We also made an effort to break down some more complex issues into simple terms, so they are understandable and actionable. Then we began discussing a concept that allowed the reader the ability to use these lessons as meeting material. There may not be one larger opportunity in our industry than our lack of quality communication and the frequency. Most know the value of a daily staff lineup but rarely exercise it across all shifts in a useful and meaningful way. When we communicate with clarity and simplicity our chances of successful execution increase exponentially.

This book was designed with the idea that just one of these lessons properly applied would pay for your time and use of the book. I asked David if he thought we had any venues that were successfully operating all these concepts at a world class level and the answer was no. It should be noted, we work with literally some of the very best bars and restaurants in the world and wanted to make sure that even in that scenario there would be something in here that even they could benefit from, we're confident we achieved that end.

As you heard Sean Finter mention in the forward, our industry is wrought with challenges and in order to defeat those challenges and find financial and emotional well-being we must be brilliant at the basics. Our aim is to make a positive impact, to leave a mark that turns the table on your odds of success. It's a fine line between winning and losing. The concepts in this book are tried and true born of the best and brightest we've encountered, and we're thrilled to share them with you. We hope you enjoy and benefit from the read, and let's go be brilliant together!

Leadership

Leadership tends to be hard to teach; in fact, many people don't believe it can be taught. I reject the idea that you cannot teach someone how to properly lead; however, I will say that you can only teach leadership to someone who is truly passionate about learning. The fact is that most people can integrate leadership skills into their strengths...if they want to. From Richard Branson, to Warren Buffet, to Carnegie, to Lincoln, many different personalities are suited for leadership. This section has been designed to give any manager who wants to learn what it really means to lead and develop a world-class team.

Leadership Pillars

"Leading people is most challenging and, therefore, the most gratifying undertaking of all human endeavors."
-Jocko Willink

It seems appropriate that we begin our book with a chapter on leadership. There are entire books written on this subject and there are several I'd like to recommend, and I will at the end of the chapter. For our part, there's a few critical touchpoints that we'd like to highlight to make sure we're all properly oriented as we share our best practices.

You see, all the content in this book will fall on deaf ears if we don't have the ability to lead. If there is such a thing as a "Magic Pill," it's leadership. Conversely, the best laid plans and concepts will collapse underneath the weight of poor leadership. So, let's review a few concepts that we must get right as leaders.

Lead by example

There's an age-old adage in the military that there are two types of leaders; one you want to put a bullet in and one you take a bullet for. Hopefully we all aspire to be the latter. We hear about leading by example and most people in management roles will tell you they do just that but in reality, it's more rare than people would have you believe. You see, leading by example isn't just a physical action such as covering a bar shift. It's also how you conduct yourself, your emotional maturity and awareness, your professionalism, and your reliability. People take their work cues from our very own behavior. For example:

If you have a reliability problem in your business check your own reliability.

If your venue is full of drama, ask yourself about how you handle drama in the culture you've built.

Basically, this is the ultimate 'look in the mirror' exercise. People take their behavior cues from their leaders; you set the tone of culture and acceptability in your business. The next piece here is action over words. Once you've built a culture, you have to fight for it. If and when people go against what you profess to be the essence of your business, your culture, and how you behave, there must be accountability. That accountability must be palpable in the business. Those who fall into the category of "all talk no action" ultimately lose control of the culture they set out to create for their bars.

Like versus respect

Years ago, I had to make the transition from employee to manager. I had the benefit of several great leaders and managers to help me with all sorts of foundational philosophies and principles to ensure I had a successful transition. One of the most important things they taught me was that it is better to be respected than liked. They further explained that when they ultimately left a position, they would rather people say, "He was tough, but I respected him" versus "I liked the guy but he wasn't all that good." For new managers this is the first real hurdle of leadership. The transition from colleague to manager is a crucial time where you'll be judged and tested. It's important to establish yourself as an authority figure without appearing to be on a power trip.

There's no way to be prescriptive here on every possibility, that's why I opt for the idea of garnering respect. People know the right answers and they will test and observe you very carefully to see if you make the right decisions. Are you consistent, reliable, and fair? These are the keys to becoming a respected leader of people. Again, there are entire books on leadership principles and we can't possibly cover all that nuance in a few pages. I advise everyone in leadership roles to keep learning, keep reading, and become an expert in your craft.

Rewards and consequences

I don't advocate for over-indexing on either side of this equation; we want to be even-handed about both rewards and consequences. It's important to recognize people's achievements, it's also important that we don't celebrate mediocrity. When we celebrate the accomplishments of average, we diminish that which is truly great in the business. The same holds true for consequences.

Ultimately, people must be held accountable. I know a lot of people in our industry who manage scared, people who fear losing staff or they let some people run wild in their business because these few staff members are seen as rainmakers. It's critical that we are consistent on both sides of this equation, we set standards, and we hold people to those standards. As a leader you'll have to make a lot of discretionary decisions about discipline and rewards. The one thing you absolutely cannot do here is ignore and avoid.

People need to be held accountable to your rules and culture.

People should be rewarded and coached based on the goals and objectives you have established for them.

If you don't already have goals and objectives for each employee, close the book, start writing them down and schedule your one-on-one's to discuss together.

Remember if you don't set specific goals for your team they will set them for themselves and they may not be in line with what you're trying to accomplish. You should have one on one meetings with your team at least once per month and discuss things like their achievements to your goals, their personal ambitions, as well as projects or special assignments they may have been given. The point is to connect with your team and have meaningful individual dialogue; this is the essence of leadership.

The power of follow-up

There's no more powerful tool in the manager's toolbox than the power of follow-up. We bring this up a lot in other chapters as well, it's that impactful. If all we do is talk but never follow up, the likelihood of people actually doing the things we require is very low.

Be sure that when you give directions you also let people know when you expect each task to be completed and then make sure you have a mechanism, like a task list, that alerts you to your responsibilities to revisit each item with your team. A lot of direction with low follow-up will lead to very low execution rates. Final note here, applying a system like this irregularly leads to reward and consequence issues relative to inconsistency. You owe it to yourself and your team to be vigilant about this process so your rewards and consequences are predictable and meaningful. The more known you become for revisiting your instructions, the more productive you will become. People will begin to do things the first time you ask them, or they will work themselves out of the business as part of your accountability program.

So, keep track of the things you assign to people and be fanatical about circling back to each one and watch how much faster you get things done in the business. Here are few management books I'd recommend to anyone looking to develop their leadership skill set, these are all easy reads.

- ✓ *"First Break All the Rules"* – Marcus Buckingham and Curt Coffman

- ✓ *"Leadership Secrets of Atilla the Hun"* – Wess Roberts

- ✓ *"Good to Great"* – Jim Collins (specifically Level 5 leadership).

- ✓ *"The One Minute Manager"* – Kenneth Blanchard and Spencer Johnson

Candor with Kindness

"Candor is the key to collaborating effectively. Lack of candor leads to dysfunctional environments."

– Ed Catmull

If we look at the spectrum of management styles in our industry we find on one end we have the 'anti-conflict' manager and on the opposite end the 'iron fist' manager.

The 'anti-conflict' manager aims for the best and values harmony over all else.

The 'iron fist' manager rules over their domain with absolutism.

In our experience the most effective management style is a hybrid of the two, which is where most people tend to reside in terms of style and approach.

It's extremely difficult to run a bar if you fear conflict and it's also nearly impossible for a brow beaten team to turn around and provide great hospitality to guests. All too often we see teams and bartenders share very openly with their guests the inner workings of the venue to include conflicts and whatever the drama of the day presents. This is clearly not a best practice as people come to our bars to escape drama and conflict. They have their own issues and the bar is their sanctuary. They don't need to hear about the internal issues of the bar. All of this is obviously unhealthy for everyone involved and sets a really poor tone for the business.

Kim Scott, Co-Founder of Candor Inc. has a great program called Radical Candor where she discusses the moral obligation; we have to be honest and coach. She tells of her experience when employed at Google where after delivering some great results in a presentation her boss had guidance she felt like she desperately needed, which included using too many 'um's' in her presentation.

"Radical candor is humble, it's helpful, it's immediate, it's in person — in private if it's criticism and in public if it's praise — and it doesn't personalize." That last P makes a key distinction: "My boss didn't say, 'You're stupid.' She said, 'You sounded stupid when you said um.' There's a big difference between the two."

Here's what we know: we must communicate clearly and often. We know we must address opportunities in the business, as well as recognize the wins and the immense amounts of positives that happen day in and day out. We have found that candor with kindness is the best way to effectively get our message across without breaking the spirit of service right before we need to go out and create amazing experiences for our guests. Here are a few recommendations on how to deliver coaching in a positive fashion without sacrificing the seriousness of the needs for the business:

- **Stay calm.** If you must use emotion, make sure it's done in a calculated fashion. **Don't rage!**

- **Use data, facts and figures.** Take opinions out of the equation if possible. Cold hard facts are indisputable and make for a great starting point for a coaching conversation.

- **Explain why the coaching matters.** Tie your coaching conversation to the necessary business outcomes.

- **Paint the picture of what good looks like.** Explain how this impacts everyone involved.

- **Get buy in.** Don't walk away from the conversation without the other person/people acknowledging the message and committing to the improvement required.

- **Follow up.** There may be no more powerful activity than follow up. Instruction without the subsequent follow up is just noise.

If you intend to coach in a group setting, reference our next chapter, **"Staff Meetings"** on how to run an effective meeting. We want to deliver this content within the construct of a productive meeting.

Staff Meetings

"Meetings are the linchpin to everything."
– Patrick Lencioni

I was thinking the other day how often I find myself saying, "You don't have a (service/liquor/food problem); you have a communication problem," which can be born of a host of issues as we all too well understand. Allow me to take a step back and share a brief story.

My management training began at a company called UPS, where I worked for nine fairly intense years. The very first thing they teach you as a new supervisor is how to conduct a proper shift meeting. It goes like this:

- Tell 'em what you're going to tell them.
- Tell 'em.
- Tell 'em what you told them.
- 1-3 topics max.
- 5 minutes max.
- Do it every day!

The overwhelming success of UPS is not by accident and very much born from disciplined communication. Our results are directly tied to our team's understanding of our expectations and outcomes. We see a lot of communication in restaurants and bars and it's most typically in the moment, "Do this/do that," born of tactical necessity. This communication shouldn't be confused for quality team meetings.

The other thing I see a lot is the polar opposite. We're having a meeting and it turns into a 20-minute ramble. After a few minutes you've lost the group. In the end people can only remember a couple of ideas presented to them in your meeting. So, to repeat, tell them what you plan to talk about, talk about it, and then confirm.

As a great test, at the end of your meeting ask people to repeat what the meeting was about or better yet have at least three people re-teach the three or less topics you covered. Keep everyone on their toes. Then be sure and use the power of follow-up to check in on people throughout their shifts to see if they are implementing the concepts presented in your meetings.

That leads me to the second thing they taught me at Big Brown.

"It takes 22 days to create a habit."

So often I hear, "Well, we told them" or "We had a meeting." One of the primary building blocks of any great operation is great communication. To maximize the impact of our message we need to repeat it until it becomes a habit. Don't think that just because you had a meeting, anything will automatically change in the business. It is rigorous follow up that will exact change in the business for you. Constant ongoing check-ins and reminders will create that impactful change you need. It may seem like a lot but in the end this will make you wildly more productive when your team is synced up with you and follows all your protocols.

One of the best by-products of being a master communicator is employee retention. The more you communicate, the more connected you become; the more connected you become, the more loyal your employees will be to you and your business. An important note: be sure to mix in the good news and outstanding accomplishments during your meetings as well, not just the latest task list.

A brief example of what this may look like:

- Good afternoon everyone! (Be enthusiastic; you're on stage for 2-3 minutes).

- Outline your two to three topics.

- I have three things to cover today: a change in the wine list, time off requests, and POS keying errors.

- Discuss your topics.

  - First, we changed the wine list to include…
  - Next, if you need time off you must follow…
  - Finally, we appreciate your feedback to adding new keys in the system and …
  - Check for understanding.
  - So, we reviewed the wine list, time off requests and POS keys.
  - Joe, what are the changes in the wine list?
  - Kirstin, describe our time off policy.
  - Rod, what are the new keys we added?

In summary, be disciplined and meet daily. Keep it short and to the point. Check for understanding and don't think just because you had a meeting anything will change in the business. Also, one-off conversations should be handled as such. If someone wants to have a discussion about a topic that has nothing to do with the group or the meeting topics of the day, handle those off-line one-on-one. If the conversation merits a full group meeting, there's always tomorrow. Don't skip days; every day we meet. Final note: It's your follow up and continued communication that will effect change for you in the business.

Time will Tell

"I'm definitely going to take a course on time management...just as soon as I can fit it into my schedule."
– Louis E. Boone

I get inspired by the things I see in venues every day. I try to make good notes in an effort to write about the most relevant topics I see that can impact you and your business. With that in mind, I can't get through a day without hearing people talk about time or the hours they work. This made me think about some things that I've been taught and have impacted my career in a positive way. I tried to distill that down to a few meaningful bullet points you can apply to your work life.

Time is such a precious commodity. We're always clamoring for more of it, running out of it or up against it. How often does your 8-hour day turn into a 12-hour day and you still don't get everything done? So often time manages us rather than us managing our time, so I thought we might look at some simple ways to improve how we organize our time.

In our industry, many people are working significant hours but largely void of an actual daily, weekly, or monthly plan for their time. I see a lot of routines; however, routines aren't to be confused with an organized effort. Routines are simply habits, good and bad, that we have built for ourselves, not necessarily a productive use of our time. We all want 'more time' but what we are actually saying is "I need to do more with the time I have." Instead I just want to focus on the idea of organizing your time wisely. Start by asking, "What do I need to accomplish and when can I do it?"

Here are five simple concepts that I hope you find helpful.

1. **Plan your work and work your plan.** Have a daily calendar and stick to it. You should, at the very least, be using the calendar features available to you on your PC, and linking them to your phone, with all your events and reminders loaded. Next, book all your events such as: expo, projects, supplier calls, interviews, staff meetings, payroll, etc. Plan all your time so you can see what you have to do and if you actually have the time in a day to do it.

    Key idea: Don't over commit yourself.

2. **Plan ahead.** You should have at least a month sketched in advanced. There's no way to build a schedule day to day and be able to manage long-term objectives and strategies of the business. Try to schedule at least a month at a time; which will flex with business needs.

Key Idea: Schedule both short-term and long-term objectives.

3. **Schedule down time.** Be sure to book empty blocks of time to deal with the unexpected, have time to think or simply converse with the boss, peers, and employees alike. If every second of your day is booked you're well over capacity. Overcapacity is ultimately unproductive. If you are going to be the best version of yourself and the most useful to others you need energy. Schedule time to recharge. As Vince Lombardi that said, "Fatigue makes cowards of us all!"

Key idea: Schedule time to think and recharge!

4. **Have discipline.** It's challenging to go from an unscheduled existence to a scheduled one. Start every day by looking at your plan and finish the same way. How did you do, what needs to be rescheduled, what's on the docket for tomorrow? It will feel rigid at first. Stick to it!

Key idea: Your time is valuable.

5. **Schedule personal time.** It's not just a work thing. Put your workout on schedule, schedule time for lunch with a friend, movie with the kids, or call your mom for goodness sake! It's also a great way to remember birthdays and anniversaries for family, friends and employees. We all get so busy it's just too easy to forget.

Key idea: Remember why we do this to begin with.

Hiring Bartenders / Staff 5

"Hospitality is almost impossible to teach. It's all about hiring the right people."

– Danny Meyer

I'm asked every week "Do you know any bartenders? We're looking for one." I almost never recommend bartenders. Why? Because concepts and culture vary so greatly those are very personal and critical business decisions. Perhaps no decision is more important than the people you bring into the business to represent you and your brand.

According to the National Restaurant Association our industry experiences, on average, a 70% employee turnover rate. That's a staggering statistic in a world that relies on each transaction to be special or at the very least meeting expectations or risk the wrath of social media.

Up next... a few tips as it relates to hiring:

- **First and foremost is hiring for attitude over aptitude.** My experience is that experience is overrated if it doesn't include a firm grasp of how to deliver a fantastic customer experience or at least your version of it. Very few people are predisposed to deliver great customer service by nature. We found about 15% of people are intrinsically motivated to give great service. What does that mean? It means no matter how bad their day, no matter how much they don't like the boss, no matter how busy they are, these people find personal fulfillment and satisfaction in serving others and nothing gets in the way of that because it's who they are, not what they do. So, in the interview process we want to ask questions that help us identify why they are in this line of work, what do they enjoy the most and what are their dislikes about the business. We're looking for people who like people, enjoy serving others, and are naturally engaging. We can teach people how to pour a beer and make a cocktail but without the desire to serve the rest just won't work.

- **Promote from within.** If you have good hiring practices throughout the organization, you should have service warriors throughout your business. Ideally, you'd be pulling servers, back of the house employees, or even hostesses up through the ranks who have a proven track record of reliability and a desire to serve. As you hire people you should be able to provide a career path for people that outlines the benefits of doing it right and how opportunities can be available to people who embrace your culture. If you're not promoting from within, you should question your hiring and development practices.

When you go external make sure you know exactly what you're looking for in the interview process. Ask open ended questions with an emphasis on why they love bartending. Their response should give you great clarity as to whether they are a good hire. Too many people interview by doing all the talking about what their expectations are for the prospect. Do yourself a favor and talk less and listen more. Ask short poignant questions about what you're interested to know and let them walk you through their view of the world. When you hire great cultural fits, these people make you more money and make your life easier, the ultimate win/win for you and the business.

- **Don't begin hiring when you have an immediate need.** Too many people begin the hiring process when they are desperate to fill shifts which leads to bad hiring decisions. You should always be developing from within and interview when you don't necessarily have an opening to avoid the desperate hires. You're always hiring and developing staff. Always.

So be slow to hire and quick to fire, protect and hire to your values. Far too many people suffer through bad hires and culture killers in fear of not being able to replace them. If you are always hiring and always developing people you will find people are much quicker to adhere to expectations because there's always someone in the wings and you're not held hostage.

Rainmaker bartenders who feel irreplaceable tend to make their own decisions about what the bar culture will be on their shift and can begin to believe they are more important than the bar. We're always in the market for service warriors who are team players and respect the opportunity that has been given to them. Anything short of that should be an opportunity to upgrade. Make sure you always have personnel options in the business.

Full Awareness

"Notice the small things. The rewards are inversely proportional."

– Liz Vassey

In case you didn't quite notice, in the first five chapters, we've largely discussed leadership as it relates to people driven events. In the proceeding leadership chapters, beginning now, you'll realize that we have begun to shift focus on matters that lean more toward process versus people leadership. As we make our end run through the first major segment of the book, let's start with a dialogue about awareness.

I was walking through my garage the other day when I noticed the wood on my outside support column had completely rotted away. I thought to myself, "Wow, how did that happen?" Then my wife told me it had been that way for two years and I'm just getting around to noticing it. I've walked past that beam every single day for two years and never noticed! I'm thinking I might hear about this one again a time or two.

Fortunately, in business I trained myself years ago to look at my team and locations anew at all times. For me, it was large distribution operations. I would walk in and ask: Were the ashtrays outside full of cigarettes? Were the trash cans clean and empty? Did the paint look fresh? Are there cobwebs on products? Are the sign postings current? You get the idea. We can become dangerously accustomed to walking right past obvious small problems simply because it's normalized for us. Teach yourself to look at your venue from the moment you arrive in the parking lot as if you're visiting for the first time.

I learned the more I noticed, the more my team would notice, and as a result, they would auto correct the things that were wrong. When they knew the expectations, they too would simply pay more attention to the details of the business and the culture of awareness improved for everyone. We, as leaders, set the pace in this regard. "Inspect what you expect," as they say. How's your awareness? Being in different venues every day we tend to notice little things like:

- The corners of the floor are not cleaned because the mop does not quite hit them easily.

- There's a light out on the sign outside.

- The pictures are hanging crooked.

- The windows haven't been clean in a while.

- Top shelf bottles are full of dust.

- Don't look under the cooler!

- Does the place smell like an old mop?

- Sticky tables and bars.

- The flower beds are full of cigarette butts.

- Server stations are full of clutter.

Here's a suggestion: When you enter your venue, think of yourself as a new customer. When we go somewhere for the first time, we tend to be hyper-aware and observant. We notice! This is how those new customers we want so badly see the business. Make sure you're seeing your business through their eyes. Challenge yourself to see your venue as a first-time customer would and ask yourself, "What do I see?" You can also make a checklist of small items that you always want to see that may not be so easy to observe, like what's under those coolers. Finally, consider mystery shop programs. They're a great way to get honest, candid feedback from a neutral party without it hitting social media first.

In our very busy world, it's so easy to fall into a speed routine that creates blinders for us. Train yourself to take the blinders off and see your venue as if it were the first time, every time!

Organization Matters

"Electricity is just organized lightning"

– George Carlin

There are many options to consider when building out a bar. Menus, type (Sports, Cocktail, Neighborhood, etc...), Social Media Strategy, Complex vs. Simple, and so on....

Organized vs. disorganized is not one of those options you should consider if one of your goals is to make money. Organization is directly related to the success of every aspect of your business.

There are many benefits, but those two are my favorites...

Organization equals Operational Efficiency: *If you get this right, you get improved customer service, happier staff, maximized revenue, and a supply chain that is easier to manage.*

Organization equals Cleanliness: *People perceive disorganization as dirty, uncontrolled, and hard to monitor. That is, a disorganized business looks (and is) easier to rip off.*

When it comes to your bar, there are 4 main areas to consider that require thought and attention when deciding how they will be set up. The one thing they all have in common is that they must be set up the same way every day if you want to make the most out of your operation.

- **Back-up Storage** - Stock your specific types and brands of spirits, beers, and wines in the same places and the same ways every time an order comes in. Depending on your volume, this may need to be addressed daily. My bar in Baltimore moved so much beer that the walk-in cooler had to be reorganized after every shift so we didn't lose any money due to hunting for a beer when we had a run on at the bar.

- **Back Bar** - The best bartenders working at the best bars don't need to look hard for what they need off the back bar. The top bartenders in the world know exactly where each product is and make sure that they control where that product lives. The most amazing thing I have ever seen was a bartender who could find products on his back bar without turning around to look.

- **Speed Rails/Well Products** - It shocks me when I meet a client who does not have a Rail that is set up the exact same way every time I visit. I have seen as many variations of order as I have seen bars; however, you want to set it based on the products used for your commonly ordered drinks.

- **Build Area** - Wherever you make your drinks and set your orders up must be orderly and have all the right tools in the right places. How you set up your build area will depend heavily on what your focus is. Cocktail venues tend to have this down to a beautifully structured system by necessity. However, every bar on the planet would benefit from a set organization for their build areas.

As with many chapters we have here, I could write an entire book on this subject alone. However, there is one last concept I want to talk about that I love and that almost no one I have met focuses on: How organization measurably impacts revenue.

When you are operating at peak trade (you can not fit any more people in the bar and every bartender is building order after order with no break) your revenue stream is measured in seconds. Don't believe that seconds matter? Then this is where the math comes in...

Let's take some nice round numbers of a properly organized bar where a well-trained bartender can make their average $10 drink in 60 seconds (including order, prep, drink build, ringing, cash out, etc...)

That bartender could ring $600 per hour in that configuration.

If that same bartender needs to hunt for tools and bottles, wait for their turn at the Point Of Sale (POS), and squeeze fresh lime juice for only an extra 15 seconds for each drink build; the impact is massive.

The extra 15 seconds per build means that they are producing the same $10 in 75 seconds instead of 60.

To see the impact, let's break that down to revenue per second:

$$\$10/60sec = \$0.167 \text{ per second.}$$
$$Vs.$$
$$\$10/75sec = \$0.1333 \text{ per second.}$$

Doesn't look like much does it? But that 15 second delay has a pretty drastic impact when we play it out over time.

$$\$0.1333 \times 60sec = \$8.00/minute$$
$$and$$
$$\$8.00/min \times 60min = \$420/hour$$

That 15 second delay costs $180 in lost revenue every single hour you're operating at peak.

Let's say you have only 5 peak hours per week (a very low estimate for most venues). That would work out to $900 per week, or $46,800 per year.

You are going to have your own delays specific to your bar, but no matter who you are, most continual and repetitive delays behind the bar are 100% free to fix; which means that that most of that $46,800 will be profit. To put it another way, if all you need to spend to fix delays caused by a lack of organization is a little thought and time then most or all of that revenue you lost would have gone straight to your profitability.

I encourage you to figure these numbers out in your business. No matter what your numbers are; which you can plug into the equations below, the revenue impact of regular and predictable delays of seconds will be massive for any bar with just a few hours of peak operation every week.

How to calculate what your team is currently capable of ringing every second at peak:

$$\frac{Retail\ Value\ of\ Average\ Drink\ Order}{\#\ of\ Seconds\ to\ build\ and\ serve\ that\ order} =$$

$$Current\ Retail\ \$\ per\ second$$

How to calculate the improvement to your revenue at peak if you identify and correct bottlenecks that are costing you precious seconds during peak operations:

$$\frac{Retail\ Value\ of\ Average\ Drink\ Order}{\#\ of\ Seconds\ after\ time\ issue\ is\ fixed} =$$

$$Improved\ Retail\ \$\ per\ second$$

Now we can use the figures from the first two equations to see what your increase in hourly revenue at peak would be:

(Improved Retail $ per Second — Current Retail $ per second)
× **3,600** *seconds per hour*
= *Hourly Revnue increase at Peak Operation*

Finally, we want to look at that figure over the course of a year:

Hourly Revenue Increase × *# of Hours at Peak Each Week*
× 52 *weeks per year*
= *Annual Return on Investment*

There are few other exercises I have worked through with clients that produce as large and reliable a return to their business. You are already packed with customers at some point, all you need to do is get a few more drinks in their hands by making your bartender's lives easier.

Social Media Management

"The best advice for anyone on social media is to be real and to be consistent. People will connect more with you if you stay true to yourself and who you are."

– Lele Pons

We have gone past a time where social media can help those savvy enough to take advantage of the way it can reach thousands of potential guests in the blink of an eye to a time where we ignore it at our peril. In this day, few can afford to go without some sort of plan or set of guidelines determining how management and staff represent their bar online.

To a great degree, bars have always lived and died on their reputation. For the longest time, a reputation was carried through print advertisements and word of mouth. Whether you pride yourself as having the divey-est, down to earth place to have a beer or the newest, hottest nightclub, you put the word out that you had the right spot and served those who walked in your doors. In the event that someone in your bar had a bad experience and you had something to do with it, you did your best in the moment and realized that the damage would be kept between them and their friends.

Facebook, Yelp, Twitter, Instagram, and whatever comes next changed all of that. Now, a simple bad experience, that you may have once considered a simple mistake that should roll off your back can devastate your client base (sometimes slowly, but make no mistake, bad reviews have an impact.)

If you are working in a venue with no real social media plan, you can create a massive impact on generating traffic by creating a well thought out and executed social media program. Even if you have a plan in place, it never hurts to have another set of eyes taking a look under the hood.

Any decent plan for social media interaction will consider two sides: Promoting the Brand and Reacting to reviews.

From you to your Clients:

Promoting your business is fairly straight forward. You need to decide the frequency, determine who is allowed to post on behalf of the business, and design a plan of what you want to post about.

Frequency: The only bad frequencies are zero and erratic. I like a minimum of a daily post; however, I have had clients do well with both multiple posts a day and as infrequent as once a week.

Who Posts: This is often overlooked and not discussed enough with staff. You do not have to look far to find people who have ruined their careers and restaurants with a poorly thought out post. No matter who you allow to post on behalf of the brand, the two rules I recommend are:

- Pick one and only one person to write official posts.
- NEVER post when drinking!

And, if you aren't sure if the post is a good idea...don't post it.

NOTE: Posting negative comments is always tricky. I have seen a few people get away with it, but more often I find it blows up in people's faces; the high ground tends to win in the public eye.

What ever shall you post? Just as with print or word of mouth promotions; the online world is pretty wide open. You can do some pretty cool stuff including posting videos on how certain dishes and cocktails are made but the four basics are:

- **Menu changes**: When you have a new menu roll out, you want to be talking about it outside of your venue as much as you do inside the venue. Post photos of the new dishes (be careful to ensure the photos are appetizing; there are many guides out there showing how to do this) talk about why you love them; ask your guests to do the same.

- **Specials:** I have a client who does a cocktail of the day, tweeting out a photo and a tantalizing description for each one. Whether it is a great food special or a lovely libation; why wait for people to walk in the door before telling them?

- **Advertising Events:** This is not a one and done post. If you have an event you want people to attend, start getting the word out at least 1 month before, and do so on multiple platforms.

- **Sharing Events:** One of the best uses of social media for anyone wanting to show off their fun time is to post photos of the events in action. Do your best to ensure that no staff is shown in compromising positions.

From them to you:

There are hundreds of thousands of reviews out there and it is shocking how many remain ignored. There are three basic principles you can follow when it comes to dealing with reviews:

- Respond to everything
- Respond only to the negative reviews
- Ignore everything

Apply the last at your peril.

I prefer the "everything" approach, however, one thing remains true for responding to any and all negative reviews; saying nothing is generally worse, but you can do so much more damage replying with indignation, anger, or other form of ignorance. Remember; while they may be right or wrong, people who post were your guests and they had an experience you would likely want to rectify.

The simplest strategy is to apologize for the bad experience, let them know that this is not the experience you intend your guests to have, and invite them back so that you can make it right. I tend to stay away from offering anything for free online, however, going above and beyond once they come back is the best way to change minds and get them to type up an addendum.

If you let negative posts fester, you will see an eventual, very real, negative impact on your business.

The last thing to consider is that social media is an extension of your restaurant. Venues that focus on creating an amazing service experience, serving the best food they can, and owning up to any mistakes they make (we are all just human here…), tend to have great reviews online. When they do get a guest griping about a bad experience in their bar, they tend to reply in the same way they would on site and work to turn the angry guest into a raving fan.

Community Involvement 9

"A true community is not just about being geographically close to someone or part of the same social web network. It's about feeling connected and responsible for what happens."

– Yehuda Berg

We wanted to dedicate a chapter to the importance and opportunity that is community involvement. Our venues provide unique opportunities to help and connect with our communities and there's so much meaningful work happening out there we can plug into.

Involvement is a dynamic concept which can include simple things like sponsoring local teams and events. We also found that there's an even more impactful way to integrate within your community. We have clients that make their venues available as meeting space for groups who may not be able to afford or have access to traditional meeting space. We also have clients that take it to another level by not only making meeting space available but also making a portion of the venue available as free event space. They learned their bar and restaurants typically had significant downtime throughout regular business hours. In fact, we know 80% of our profits are made in 20% of our operating time. So, consider driving more activity into that 80% where you have vast amounts of bandwidth with very little revenue opportunity. This is where we can do community outreach. Typically, nonprofit organizations are willing to be very flexible in exchange for free space.

Your bar can turn into the best meeting place in town! There's food, drink, TV, music and aesthetics - with what other meeting place can we get such luxuries? Yet, very few venues make full use of their space in this capacity. Now, we're not booking these charitable events during peak trade hours. Leverage your availability needs with theirs and you'll find all sorts of unexpected opportunities. You must also be sure to advertise the fact that your space is available for meetings and charitable events and consider what sort of menu options and/or drink specials you make available to the group. People are always looking for great meeting space; the key is to make sure your availability is known and broadcast your availability as meeting space.

Our clients who are successful in this regard tell us when they make themselves open to helping their communities, their communities respond in kind. People don't forget good works and service. Remember, it is hard to be the neighborhood bar if you're not involved in your neighborhood. It's not enough just to say the words, you must get involved and be a part of the social fabric that is your community. This will yield huge dividends on the revenue side of the business. Of course, we don't do good works with revenue expectations, but it is a very real benefit. It's okay to give a little to get a little in return when our intentions are right and we serve as a positive force in our communities.

Bar Operations

It's the little details that make or break most bars and for that matter most businesses. As an industry, we tend to get wrapped up in the urgent and miss out on a whole host of good intentions prior to the shift beginning. As the age-old adage goes "The devil is in the details" so true!

Out of necessity, you will get the urgent handled. The key becomes getting those critical seemingly mundane processes to an easily executable place using your talents and the talents of those around you, while still managing all those urgent needs that are bound to pop up each shift. In the following chapters we will supply you with a whole host of ideas and strategies that will help you become a more efficient operator.

The Menu

"When you do a menu at a restaurant, you have to be the engineer of that menu. It has to be a crowd-pleaser."
– Jean-Georges Vongerichten

S imple but not basic is a good place to start. As we will discuss in Chapter 11 – **"Decision Paralysis"** and Chapter 12 – **"Is Free Really for Me"** on how free items impact your venue. Keeping your bar orderly and simple to understand should translate perfectly to your menu. Let's explore some ways to help you accomplish this goal.

According to the National Restaurant Association's State of the Industry Research, customers are 70% more likely to choose one venue over another if and when they have healthy and/or locally sourced options. That's a pretty telling statistic. 'Buy local' has become a new hallmark of our industry. In addition, 85% of operators in the same data set believe that customers are more knowledgeable now than they were just two years ago.

Let's start with beer, always a good place to begin! There was a time when having five to eight draft options available was considered normal and that selection was usually very predictable and limited and rarely included a local craft option. Now there are so many bottle and draft options that some venues actually rotate their selection daily. Product assortment will only continue to diversify so we need to systematize our menu in a way that's not confusing to our guests. So how do we do that? We recommend breaking down your offering by taste preference. We know people like to traditionally break down menus by local, domestics, and imports. We prefer to break down by flavor profiles such as IPA's, wheat/wit, porters, lagers, ales, etc. Typically, we don't have more than a handful of each of these on our menu. Most people know what type of beer they enjoy drinking, so by breaking down our menu by profile type we give our guests the simplicity of selection while still offering a diverse menu. Driving clarity for your guest in an environment of growing complexity is always a good thing and can even be a competitive advantage. Within your menu break down you can include other source location information. Guests often enjoy small tidbits about their selection such as ABV, flavor profiles, and source location.

It's also a good menu practice to drive attention to your promotions. Make sure you make good use of inserts or have secondary and even tertiary menus that emphasize seasonal offerings and specials. I can't tell you how many times we see clients create specials they really want to move and are doing absolutely nothing in terms of promoting their ideas.

We very much like the idea of using these same concepts with bourbons, whiskeys, scotch, vodka, gin and wines. Depending on the extent of your offerings you may opt for a dedicated wine list and the same may be true for cocktails if you're a cocktail bar or offer a wide variety of unique cocktails.

In the end, your menu should be easy to traverse, allow the guest to get right to what they enjoy, and make an easily informed decision. This is obviously good for the guest experience and it's also good for staff productivity. It is more common than not that we find venues carry far more product than what they advertise or communicate. A good rule is: if you carry a product on your bar, not including mixers, you should have a plan to sell it. This should include them being a part of the menu and having a key in the POS (see Chapter 18 – **"Keys are the Key"**).

So remember, keep it simple, advertise your specials, and if you have a lot of diversity in your products parse out your menu by flavor profiles and product types. Your menu should be easily digestible.

Decision Paralysis

"A good decision is based on knowledge not numbers."

- Plato

What is decision paralysis? By definition it would be: The state of over-analyzing (or over-thinking) a situation so that a decision or action is never taken, in effect paralyzing the outcome. So what does this mean for our industry? Well, recently I was in a bar with 362 taps and guests simply became overwhelmed with choices. Now most of you won't have 362 taps; however, you may be surprised at how little it takes for guests to become overwhelmed in the decision-making process; which ultimately renders your massive investment in selection useless. This also happens in bars with massive alcohol selections or venues that use products as "decoration" to fill space behind the bar to be aesthetically pleasing.

When people become overwhelmed by options they will instinctively go to their 'safe place' and back to a basic drink that they are comfortable with. After all no one goes to a bar to be uncomfortable. This is typically the exact opposite behavior we are looking to achieve. We want to deliver a unique experience through our offerings, yet we unwittingly chase people into their safe space.

Be mindful of our presentation of products. Sometimes less is more and if we're going to go heavy with product presentation such as 20+ taps, 10+ vodkas, etcetera we need to present our products in a way in which guests can consume the information and make an informed decision with confidence and not become overwhelmed with options.

A good place to check and see if you are in a decision paralysis state is to ask your bartenders and servers if they can tell you what you're selling. When you have such variety that the staff can't even explain what's on your shelves, it's a rare day that a guest will understand either which just leads to experience issues as well as inventory issues.

Our bartenders need to be well versed in our offerings. Many times, in the case of draft beer we will default to using samples as opposed to being able to describe our beer selection. Ideally, we can describe a beer such that a sample is unnecessary. More on this in Chapter 20 – **"The Proper Pour"** and Chapter 13 – **"Sample This!"**. Most typically, if your bartender can't describe it, they can't sell it. Go take a look at your bar and check your presentation. Evaluate all the unknown products and either get them off your bar or educate yourself and your team on the use of those products.

Final note: I see a lot of venues who don't keep their menu current with their products offering. Be disciplined about the products you bring into the venue, especially the free stuff that suppliers will drop on you. I'm not a fan of people making their slow-moving stock your slow-moving stock, also read Chapter 12 – **"Is Free Really for Me"**. So if you're going to carry it, have it priced, on the menu, and in the POS. Be sure your menu includes a good beer (draft and bottle), liquor, wine and cocktail list as well. There seems to be no letup in new craft beers. We have clients that offer well over 50 crafts on tap and that many yet again in a bottle. Some people like to have their beer list split by local, domestic, and import. I prefer beer list more like a wine list and split by their flavor profile: IPA, wheat, session, lager, stout, and pilsner etcetera. This allows people to be a little more confident in what they order and prevents you from being sampled to death as well.

To recap, the more you stock and display, the more you need to inform your guests and make sure you team knows and understands your offerings. Be certain your menu and POS are keeping pace with your stocking decisions and you should be able to defeat decision paralysis.

Is Free Really for Me?

"If someone tries to give you something for free, the first question should always be, how much does this cost?"

– Ari Schwartz

I'm constantly amazed at the amount of product proliferation we see in venues today as we discussed in Chapter 11 – **"Decision Paralysis."** The job of distributors is to introduce you to new products and keep you abreast of current industry trends, as well as ensuring you're getting the best possible deal on products. This combined effort often leads to 'free' products and offers introduced to you and your venue. Now, different markets can be unique in how they distribute alcohol, and laws definitely vary state to state and country to country. In this chapter, we're really focusing on the markets where distributors will provide free or deeply discounted products in hope to garner shelf space for new products and promotions.

I hear a lot of people say, "Well, I'm not going to turn down free booze." When I hear people say that I cringe a little as the old adage "nothing is free" is as true today as it's ever been. In contrast, we would never take up space in our kitchen with free food, we wouldn't confuse our customers by talking about product not on the food menu, and we wouldn't confuse our kitchen staff about what to make or our wait staff on how to promote it. Yet, we do this constantly with liquor. All too often new products get introduced to a venue void of any comprehensive plan on how to sell or promote them. They simply appear at the bar with the idea that somehow they will magically sell themselves.

Unplanned product takes up valuable space at bars and in stock rooms. It typically just sits there as we accumulate more and more product that doesn't necessarily fit our venue or guest experience strategy. Remember, nothing good happens from stagnant inventory. Only when we sell product do we actually benefit from having it. We've had a lot of conversations with distributors about how to integrate with venues to ensure they give thought to their new products and how they may support a venue when introducing new products. Meaning, a local sports bar may not need the new high-end wine but very much be interested in a new brewery brought on board. We also discuss the need to have a go-to market or 'guest experience' strategy for new spirits. There are so many product offerings out there today that if we don't have a cohesive plan for how we introduce new spirits to a venue it will certainly remain stagnant and eventually fail, leaving you with more dead stock in the venue. Dead stock has very little benefit. It typically involves deep discounts or becoming employee gifts at holiday season.

If new products are to take root and generate fruit there are a few steps that must be followed for there to be a chance of success. The beauty of this is that when we follow these steps we drive alignment from distribution all the way to the guest experience, which maximizes productivity and guest experience.

So here are five simple bullet points for introducing new products to your venue.

- **Have an approval process.** We don't want stuff just showing up on invoice, even if it's free of charge. As much as we like our distributors, they can't be the ones who determine what inventory changes are going to happen in the venue.

- **Insist on promotional support.** If you are to give products your bar real estate, that should include a certain measure of support from your distributor.

- **Track performance on new items.** How is the product doing and how might it be impacting other products? Are we adding new sales or are we simply cannibalizing others?

- **New product introductions should coincide with menu updates and POS set up.** Coincide new products and promotions 30-45 days before your new menu roll-out so your products and menus are integrated. Avoid confusing your guests and bartenders. Be sure to read Chapter 18 - '**Keys are the Key'** for more detail.

- **Seek out guest feedback.** It's a great best practice to discuss your new offering with your guests and see how they like it. This will help you refine your approach to introducing new products.

Sample This

"Be so read in on your draft program that you can describe your products in such a way that I can taste it."

– This guy!

Craft beers are all the rage today and there's no end in sight. There seem to be new breweries popping up every month with new and inventive flavors being introduced weekly. We're seeing some very interesting and costly trends building across craft draft performance; which I would like to share with you.

Most people won't simply buy a pint of that Chocolate Tuna IPA without trying a sample first. This leads to "death by a thousand cuts" in your draft program. I recently witnessed a venue that sold just one pint of a new craft beer, yet 40% of the keg had been disbursed. Where did all the beer go you ask? Let's find out…

- Do you rotate out crafts without verifying if they were actually worth keeping on tap? We see popular beers rotated out for unpopular ones on a regular basis because no one is tracking sales performance.

- People sample but often don't buy. Is this factored into your costs? (See Chapter 20 - **'The Proper Pour'** for a deeper dive on this.)

- Are you tracking your samples? Do you have a sample key? If yes, how is the conversion of samples to pints?

We often see crafts with losses around 30-40% due to samples coupled with standard foaming issues. If it's a seasonal or rotating tap, you may only sell through 2 or 3 kegs before you swap out. If this is the case, you can never recover the loss on that initial keg of beer.

A few things to contemplate for your business:

- Create sample keys.
- Measure and evaluate craft performance.
- Consider bringing in crafts as bottles first, evaluate sales then convert to draft.

- Don't suggest samples; let the customer ask. Who turns down free beer if offered?
- Be capable of describing the beer instead of free samples. (Also see Chapter 11 – **'Decision Paralysis.'**)
- Manage supplier enthusiasm for adding unique crafts into your venue.
- Remember crafts are already more expensive per keg prior to additional loss being built in…contemplate this as you set your pricing and evaluate performance.

How's this Sound?

"One good thing about music, when it hits you, you feel no pain."

– Bob Marley

Think back to the last song you chose to listen to or your favorite song. Why did you choose that song? How did it make you feel? Did it change your overall mood?

- Music will control your mood.

- Music will set an atmosphere.

- The Wrong Music will completely ruin an experience.

There are two bars I go to where it works that the staff is allowed to play whatever soundtrack to their life they are feeling at the time. There is no specific theme or atmosphere that defines the music played there; you connect to the staff working at that moment through their musical selection. That same setup ruins the entire experience at most other venues and when I encounter it, I rarely return.

Combine this emotional connection to music with the simple, but well understood concept that consistency breeds loyalty, and you have to realize that it is so important to carefully design your music program, rather than let your staff choose whatever Pandora channel they think should work in your bar. Human beings crave consistency. The average person wants to go to a place they know will be a certain way at a certain time with the same food, drinks, people, experience...every time.

Now don't think your job with the music stops with setting your theme song. There is a time and place for music levels that cause the "What?" "Whaaaaat?" conversation; however, that is not most times, and not most places. It is just as important to understand when your tunes should seamlessly blend into the background, becoming more atmosphere than anything else and when the levels should start coming up to a point where most people are noticing and actively thinking "Oh Man, I LOVE that song!"

You are not selling food. You are not selling booze. You are not selling somewhere to sit. You are selling an experience, be sure to also read Chapter 26 – **"Building a Bar Community"**. The food, the booze, and the service all tie into the overall experience, but so does the music; and music is emotion.

People are going to connect to your venue emotionally and decide if they want to come back whether you like it or not. They are going to decide if they want to KEEP coming back day after day; year after year. There are many parts of your experience that you can manage to control that emotion. There are none that will elicit an emotional response like music.

Think about the atmosphere you want to create, the emotion you want to connect to, the client you want to attract, and make that musical style your policy. Not every bar on the planet should loop Journey's "Don't Stop Believing'", but for the right bar, that song will create customers for life.

Cleanliness

"Cleanliness is the hallmark of perfect standards and the best quality is the conscience."

– J.R.D. Tata

Have you ever sat down at a restaurant or bar prepared to enjoy your meal or drink and the silverware made you question whether you made a good destination choice? How often have you bellied up to the bar only to have your elbows stick to the bar top? Ever get a wine glass with the remnants of lipstick around the rim? These subtle but important cues inform your customers on just how serious you are about their care as a guest.

As we discussed in Chapter 6 – **"Full Awareness"** we need to train ourselves and our staff to look for these service and cleanliness cues to avoid an embarrassing circumstance.

Throughout a guest's experience we send signals about our level of seriousness as it relates to their care. This happens in a number of ways and begins with our greeting, as we indicate in Chapter 24 – **"Hostess with the Mostess"**, all the way through check collection and departure, which we discuss in Chapter 34 **"What's Going on Here?"**. I contend that cleanliness is among the most important factors in a guest's experience. If the glassware or silverware is dirty then what must the kitchen look like? What else may my food or drink be exposed to? An unclean environment sets off a series of internal questions that we simply don't want our guests asking.

Cleanliness must be ensured!

What do best practices look like? We should never leave a dirty bar, seating area, table tops, or dishes overnight for the next shift. Each shift should inherit a clean and orderly workspace. As part of our bar opening procedure, verifying these facts should also ensure we have ourselves in the best position to give an amazing guest experience.

I strongly recommend having a bar open and bar close checklist for your bartenders; which we discuss in detail in Chapter 17 – **"Check Yourself"**. It can be very easy at the end of a late night to forget a small detail or closing activity. When we try to memorize or simply count on the team to execute, especially late night, it's far too easy to forget something. So, a simple checklist can provide you a level of accountability from your team and create a great hand-off to the AM bar staff. This is also a good place to leave other administrative notes that the team may want to leave such as "out of well rum" so it also serves as a great shift turnover tool.

Also teach your Bartenders to inspect glassware prior to preparing drinks. It should become a habit to quickly check the rim and bottom of the glass for any remnants that may not have been cleaned in the dishwasher. I would also suggest that they do the same thing as glasses are put away from the dishwasher, this is the best time to catch a cleanliness problem. One more note on glassware- if your glassware is scarred and scratched, replace it. Nobody enjoys drinking out of a glass that looks like it's been around since the First World War.

If you're wondering just how clean your venue is, a good place to start is the bottom of your coolers. If the bottom of your coolers are full of pull tabs, caps, lime and lemon wedges, rust, and swill, then you have work to do. Make sure your shelves aren't full of dust and your bottles aren't sticky. Make sure you clean your pour spouts regularly and have your spigots professionally cleaned. All this left unattended is gross at best and unsanitary at worst, and in no way represents genuine hospitality. Being a great host means we take care of the seen and the unseen aspects of our bars.

In the end, a culture of cleanliness is of vital importance to our industry and our guest experience. It is also crucial to any health inspections you may have in your area. There may be no more crippling occurrence in our business than a failed health inspection. I've been in cities where failed health inspections are covered by the local news. People aren't given the details of the failure, simply that there was one. Some of these issues are simple easy fixes and other can be more serious. Sadly, people tend to assume the worst with failed inspections and it can cripple a business. Ultimately, keep your bar clean and orderly to avoid any of these highly negative circumstances. Use checklists and inspect the unseen and out of mind areas of your bar on a regular basis. Trust but verify!

Why You Buggin'?

"Time flies like an arrow; fruit flies like a banana."
– Groucho Marx

Nobody likes a fruit fly problem. The severity of the issue often goes unnoticed until you open in the morning turn on the lights and watch as these guys run for the hills. Fruit flies ransack drains and dirty crevices before eventually drowning themselves in liquor bottles. A seemingly minor annoyance until the inevitable pour of a fly corpse into a customer's cocktail. Nobody wants that extra protein in their cocktail. What to do?

Here is a short must do list to help fight off these little bar terrorists!

- Clean. I mean really clean everything. Your rails, bottles, pour spouts, drains, and sinks. This includes that "stuff" in the bottom of your coolers. Your shelves are just as important. There are far too many shelves left out of sight out of mind when it comes to cleaning.

- Cover up all your pour spouts. People have found all kinds of different ways to keep fruit flies out of their bottles. I recommend the rubber end caps to wire shelving units, or paper medicine cups as a cheaper alternative. Execute every night, covering every bottle.

- Fans. Fruit flies aren't the strongest creatures so keep your fans on overnight at the bar and pointed towards your liquor.

- There are enzyme-based cleaning fluids you can use to pour down your drains which is a great practice for bar close every night.

- Put all your fruits and food away and keep them well wrapped.

This is my cautionary list:

- UV light: These are ok in that they are a post-problem solution, not preventative, and can become unsightly if not maintained.

- Fly traps: These seem to get forgotten about except by your customers who will notice them once they become a disgusting display of a mass grave.

- Cocktail traps: Mix up a nice sweet cocktail, cover it up in cellophane, and in they go and out they don't. Pardon me if I don't want that glass in the future. This one tops the most disgusting solution list.

` What do we recommend when you do find protein in a liquor bottle? Well you dump it of course! I know, I know, it's expensive. Look, straining it and serving it is dicey. It's literally impossible to get all the bug remnants out. Would you serve it to your mom? This is always a good test when contemplating a bad decision. The best practice is to spill the bottle and learn the lesson: an ounce of prevention is worth a pound of cure.

Go get those buggers!

Check Yourself

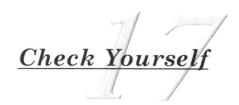

"I watch a lot of astronaut movies…mostly Star Wars. And even Han and Chewie use a checklist."

– Jon Stewart

For any occupation or process executed in a high stress environment, that has any degree of difficulty, and has around 10 steps or more to keep track of, a checklist is necessary to ensure regular success. Managing a bar is the very definition of a high stress, difficult job with hundreds of little moving parts that cannot be forgotten or skipped.

On January 15, 2009, for the first time in human history, US Airways flight 1549 struck an entire flock of geese. Unfortunately, due to the complexity and chaos of the situation, the pilot, Chesley "Sully" Sullenberger was unable to regain control. All 155 souls were lost as the Airbus A320 struck the Hudson River nose first and broke apart.

If you ask Sully, he will tell you that the above story did not end with such a tragic ending because of the checklists in his cabin that he was trained extensively to use in the event of an emergency.

"Checklists are a simple, inexpensive intervention that can formalize best practices when used properly—with leadership, team skills and in the appropriate culture…
It's not the list itself that's so effective. The list is simply a way to focus individual intention toward group goals. It's a way of formalizing best practices. It's a way of literally getting everyone on the same page"
-Chesley Sullenberger

By the time of the *Miracle on the Hudson*, one of my favorite books, *The Checklist Manifesto* by Atul Gawande, was getting ready for publication. Dr. Gawande, sickened by the seemingly unnecessary number of deaths in hospitals, turned to the lessons from the World War 1 B-17, the first aircraft to get a checklist. Dr. Gawande realized that if a checklist could allow highly skilled pilots to master the exceedingly complex craft, they should be able to reduce death by infection in hospitals.

Preventing 43 infections, 8 deaths and achieving a 0% infection rate (down from 11%) in one year of implementation at the prestigious Johns Hopkins Hospital proved him correct.

The basic premise is this: No matter how well you are trained, no matter how smart you are, the human brain can only remember a limited number of steps at a time in fast paced situations.

- Keep the language simple - this is not a guide book; it is a set of reminders to make sure you do not miss anything critical.

- Keep each item description as short as possible.

- Each list should be no more than 1 page - More lists are better than long lists.

- Checklists are living documents; Review, revise; Review, revise; Review, revise…ad nauseam.

Our industry is full of people understandably overwhelmed by a chaotic environment we all love to hate. Just like the doctors who fought against Dr. Gawande's lists for years (he had to prove his theory under substandard conditions in remote areas of Africa), we tend to feel that we are smart enough, trained enough, experienced enough to do our jobs effectively, no matter what a shift may throw at us. The reality is that we also benefit greatly from well designed and implemented checklists.

- Opening duties
- Closing duties
- Cleaning duties
- Cashing out
- Handling upset guests

These are just a few examples the reality is that any process that has more than 5 steps will fail more often than you need unless you have a strong a checklist created for it.

Keys are the Key

"Data is a tool for enhancing intuition."
– Hilary Mason

Let's talk best in class for a moment. The very best in the business track every product they sell, in every form they sell it. When you do this and create information on loss and usage and take it back to the staff the financial impact is powerful. As an example, the top 1% go so far as to track and cost their draft samples in their POS. Imagine the gap of understanding and profit between managers tracking every single sample poured by product versus those with a generic $3 Happy Hour Draft key.

Whether you're managing your liquor inventory with the old-fashioned point system or if you're using a state-of-the-art vendor to do it, you must ensure you have amazing data integrity. This begins with your POS keys. Think for a moment, do you have $3 bottle, $5 draft, domestic bucket, or generic red wine button in your POS? If so, there is absolutely no way for you to reconcile those transactions against the product that was actually served.

What's even worse are open keys which are the devil, and modifiers, which I view as the devil's son. To be clear, when I say modifiers I am talking only about when they don't "attach" in the sales file and instead report as a separate line item. Open keys and modifiers can't be reconciled back to any particular product which means you will have absolutely no idea what was sold when you use them. When you look at your Product Mix (PMIX) these two items have no connection to the inventory used. Here's a quick trick to validate your inventory awareness: if you're counting inventory and doing reconciliation for variance, you must show a higher inventory loss if you have a high open key and modifier usage. If you show little loss with high open key usage, your process doesn't work and you're failing yourself.

If we peel that back further, how do you then know what your loss is and what to manage? At that point all you're doing with inventory is determining what needs to be ordered versus what needs to be managed and corrected. In fact, you can actually start to order more product due to what was lost, not what was actually sold, and now you are negatively impacting your cash flow and profits.

Moreover, do you have keys for your ups, extras, and doubles mapped to a specific product? If I want a Lemon Drop but I request call versus well, how do you track that product usage specifically? Are you aware of product variance and how you may see an artificial increase in well inventory and an off-setting loss in premium products which creates a net loss of profit margin? If so, go to the head of the class!

Final note, everything gets rung. This includes comps, spills, discounts, and so on. People tend to get very lazy about ringing these items in, I mean, if it's free why does ringing it matter? Well, we need to track and measure our comps and compare our known loss to our unknown loss. So we should be as passionate about ringing in comps as we are ringing in our regular sales, we always want great data so we make informed decisions in the business.

Our POS and the keys therein are the gateway to understanding.

Usually your bartenders know what's not in your system so an easy way to test how effective you are at maintaining your system is to simply ask them. Also, run a product mix report and see how many open keys you have and how many generic sales are represented. That will give you a quick glimpse into how you're doing.

So, be sure to have all the right keys and reconcile your sales and losses. Final note: stay clutter free like we further discuss in Chapter 23 - **'Nothing Lasts Forever'**. When you no longer carry a product make sure you delete it from the system. Avoid clutter and confusion in your POS. All this will also make it easier for your staff to get it right the first time and maximize profits in your business!

The Draft Conundrum

"It's the little details that are vital. Little things make big things happen."

- John Wooden

When you look at the price per unit, draft beer looks like a money- making machine. Sadly, the reality is that many draft programs don't even break even, quite the opposite, they are giant money drains. There are quite a few factors that push draft programs into the red, and most of them are hidden from bar and restaurant operators. This does not mean that it is impossible to make great margins on draft beer, however, there are several moving pieces that must be taken into account during planning and then monitored every single day of operation. These next three chapters will set you up for success with your draft program experiences.

The Set up: Getting the correct theoretical cost on draft goes beyond breaking down the wholesale cost of a keg. Most bar owners know there are added costs; few have the time to work them out. These costs will wipe out that super profitable pint. There is much more detail in Chapter 20 – **"The Proper Pour"**.

The Build out: For long draw systems, if you go cheap, you risk perpetual issues in losses. A system that will keep your losses tight costs around $1,000 per draft line. A quality draft system pouring 100% perfect every pour takes about 10 kegs to break even. ($1,000/$0.70 NP per beer). If you bought a venue with a pre-existing system, never assume the previous owner knew what they were doing. You will need to pay someone, possibly top dollar, to make sure it is in peak operating condition.

Ongoing Operations: From equipment maintenance to proper pouring procedure, there are many things that fight against the profitability of draft beer.

Bad Pouring Practice: There is one right way to pour a beer. (There are countless videos on YouTube) Once you are aware of this, you will see it executed so rarely. Pulling the tap handle with no glass underneath is the most common incorrect process I see along with pouring foam off the top of the pint to drain off foam...crazy right? Make sure your team knows that every drop of beer should end up in the glass.

Pour service Time: Depending on your process, systems, and bar layout, the time to serve a draft pint can vary; however, it will always take more time to serve draft than a bottle of beer. This compounds when you are looking at serving multiples of the same beer as you can quickly pop open 4 beers one after another while you must wait for each beer to pour from a draft system one after another.

Managing Line Break Downs: This is the single largest killer in the profitability of a draft program. In one of the simpler parts of a draft system, your beer "faucet", there is an average of 12 parts that will wear out. When they do, you will start losing beer at an alarming rate. Having a strong action plan for foam and leaks is step 1, step 2 is making sure every barback, server, bartender, and manager are well trained on that plan. A single major issue can bleed your monthly draft profits in a single day.

Equipment Maintenance: While line break downs seem almost inevitable, proactivity will definitely reduce the number of times your lines decide to stop working each year. Those same lovely line systems have a lot of moving parts, valves, and gaskets that wear out over time. Find yourself a good company to clean them up and replace wearing parts on a regular basis. The amount of beer you serve will determine how often you need to do this.

If you find yourself catching one of these operational processes poorly executed in your bar or if you are aware that your draft program was never properly set up, do not fret, there are more sections to follow that will help get you back on the right track.

The Proper Pour

"There is no such thing as a bad beer. It's that some taste better than others." – Billy Carter

If I haven't scared you off from draft beer yet, you now have to consider the short and long-term costs as you decide how to proceed with your program. This may feel redundant with the last chapter, but it is important to look at draft programs from different angles.

There are major sections to consider; the equipment and the considerations for pricing out your pints. The first tends to be a one-time consideration while the ongoing pricing of your pints is where the ongoing considerations come into play.

Factoring in the one-time cost of draft equipment is fairly simple. There are two basic configurations most have to choose from - Direct draw (kegerators) and Long draw (Keg room, lines, and the such). For most, the decision of which to use comes down to space and cost. Direct draw takes up considerable space at the bar, but it's much cheaper to purchase. Long Draw generally takes up considerably more space and is more expensive, but the kegs can be kept anywhere on the property where you have space. The basic recommendation I have for either of these is this: This is not the area to go cheap.

Setting up for Success: Most of the following considerations are for the long draw systems as they are much more complex than the direct draw systems. The difference in initial price can range from $3,000 to $30,000+

- **Glycol Lines:** Beer HATES temperature changes. Fortunately, it is no longer 1930 and Glycol cooling systems are available to you! This is a must for any profitable draft system.

- **Fob Stops:** These Stop the flow of beer the moment a keg kicks, prevent spitting beer at the taps, and keep the line filled with cold beer between changed kegs. Combined with a glycol system, this will save you thousands of dollars a year in lost product.

- **Individual line Pressure regulators:** Gone are the days of "Regular or Lite?" Craft beer is currently the only growing beer category and many times, each craft on your lines will need a different pressure to pour properly.

- **The best install company in your area:** The best way I know to do this is to ask around to your "competition" about who built their system and how the build-out experience was as well as how it has held up. Don't be shy here, most Managers and Owners I know are awesome people who love helping others be successful. Beyond that, it just isn't worth getting burned.

Pricing out the pints: Getting the correct theoretical cost on draft goes beyond breaking down the wholesale cost of a keg. Most bar owners know there are added costs; few have the time to work them out. These costs take the super profitable pint much closer to its bottled brethren and so will directly impact the price you need to charge. With my clients, I generally start with questions; and there are oh so many questions when you are discussing a draft program.

What size "pint" glass are you offering? Will you be offering high octane beers that require a different, smaller glass? How will your guests perceive your pricing and pouring strategy? Will they buy what you are selling? How will you deal with the massive cost difference between the different keg sizes? Many ⅙ barrels of a beer will cost double the price per pint of the ½ barrel for the same product. How do you stack up against your competition? Does your staff know how to sell each of your beers and justify their price points? There is a lot to consider.

- **Glassware:** Draft programs are heavily dependent on price per unit. You have to ensure that your glassware is exactly the volume you planned for and don't forget to take the head into account. Higher octane beers will require a smaller glass (to make money and insure people don't get hit too hard with alcohol all at once) Additionally, you will need to measure your glassware to verify the supplier quote is accurate, See Chapter 22 **"Glassware."**

- **Competitive Pricing Point:** As a guide, the easiest way to know what the customers in your market will bear is to research what your successful competitors are doing. Worst case, this will give you a decent starting point.

- **Pricing Perception:** Perception is everything. If guests think your beer costs too much; you'll have a hard time creating repeat business. Many people would find it hard to swallow the $18/pint you would need to charge in order to make decent margins on a $300 sixtel of beer. You have to take into account what your average customer will find reasonable to pay.

- **Keg Sizes:** If you are working solely with ½ barrels you are good to go. However, ⅙ barrels of the same beer will often cost double the price per pint of the ½ barrel for that product. The key is to price each pint out based on the exact cost of each individual keg.

- **Pint by Pint Operating Costs:** This is where most draft programs come off the rails. A few initial issues can kill your program before you even get going.

    o If you are offering tastes, factor them into your costs; they add up fast.

    o If you will be rotating beers, you need to factor the cost of bleeding your lines each time you change a keg.

- **Line Cleanings:** Adding to the operating costs, line cleanings should happen once every two weeks if you want your beers to pour and taste right. On top of the hard cost, you need to take into account the 32oz to 128oz per line you will be dumping every two weeks. (remember - 1,984oz per ½ barrel keg) Very few businesses take this into account when looking at the cost of their draft program.

- **Specials:** This applies anywhere in a beverage program, but draft is one of the most commonly discounted categories. As you are operating, you will need to track how many of your drafts are bought at Happy Hour prices and make sure they are not cannibalizing the entirety of your profits.

Beer Lines

"If something isn't working the way it should, no matter how small, chances are it's going to grow into a bigger problem."

- Unknown

As we discussed in Chapter 19 - **'The Draft Conundrum,'** on paper draft is a money maker; however, draft lines are often the trickiest part to manage. The reality is that even if you have a well thought out and carefully budgeted program, many draft programs barely break even and just as many bleed cash. Beer is finicky and draft lines are complex; it takes knowledge, training, and constant monitoring to create and run a program that runs smoothly. Among the litany of issues that can lead you to the industry average of 20% loss, the following are some of the most common I have found over the years:

- Cracked seals allowing air into the line; creating foam.

- Seemingly minor temperature variations; creating foam.

- Kegs not being allowed to settle and come to temperature; creating foam.

- Staff not reporting foaming issues.

- Bad pouring technique, dumping profits down the drain.

- Equipment failing in such a way as to dump beer in between walls or into drains.

- Kegs getting untapped before they are empty.

For any of the issues you may face, the key is to give your front line a way to communicate them to you. A log book behind the bar gives the staff a place to record when there are issues so you can identify patterns and find solutions.

These are the most common issues you will face and a guide to getting a little closer to exactly what is causing your specific issues.

Temperature: Draft beer hates temperature change and 2 or 3 degrees can create massive foaming issues. The best practice here is to be proactive, checking the temperatures of the following areas no less than twice daily. To be considered are:

- **Cooler** - Most coolers have an external gauge sensor at the door, providing artificially high readings. Make sure to add 1 or 2 other thermometers throughout the cooler where your kegs are stored.

- **Glycol Bath** - There should be a digital readout that is easy to see. Your install company should be able to tell you what temperature the bath should be.

- **Tower and Tap (Faucet)** - If you get foam for the first pours of the day; this is a likely culprit. Make sure that the glycol lines go all the way to the end of the line at the tap.

Outside Air: The tiniest amount of outside air introduced into a line can destroy your ability to pull a pint. These are the most common ways for air to get into the line. Contributors are:

- **Cracks in Gaskets/O-rings and crud in the connection** - There are a few main gaskets on the tavern head and keg that can be checked for cracks once you have ruled out temperature.

- **Nicks in line** - These can be harder to detect and will require you to do a physical inspection of all of the lines connected to the keg in question.

- **Worn out tavern heads** - Once the tavern head is off the key and completely closed, there should be no beer spray, bubbling, or air hissing.

The Keg Itself: They seem like indestructible beer hugging tanks. That may be so, but their contents are still fickle and require some considerations. You need to keep on top of the following:

- **Settled/rested** - Most kegs need to settle and come to temperature for 24 hours after delivery before being tapped. Try not to jostle them too much right before you tap them.

- **Set at the correct Pressure** - Especially for certain craft beers, the proper pressure is necessary. Each system is different and it is best to get an expert in to help set up your lines.

All that information is great, but it is useless without the answer to the question: What do you do when a draft line starts foaming? This is oddly a question that most owner and management teams don't answer for their staff. If you don't have one, make a plan and whatever it is, make sure all staff is well trained on it. For my team, it was - The moment there is an excessive foam issue, cap the line and communicate the issue to a manager. Management would then deal with it. I would rather have to tell a guest that a particular beer is unavailable for a time than for my bar staff to waste product and time trying to mess around with what was more often a complex issue they can't solve at the moment.

Glassware

"Man is a tool-using animal. Without tools he is nothing, with tools he is all."

— Thomas Carlyle

Glasses are just glasses right? It took me a long time to learn the lesson that getting the right glassware for your bar can have major impacts on perception and profitability. I now pass that knowledge along to you in minutes. There are two things you can control when you are selecting glassware for your business and while it seems so innocuous to many, you definitely want to put thought into both of them.

The Look - I am no artist; however, I still find it painfully obvious when someone has not put thought into what their glasses look like. Best case, it is distracting. Worst case it can ruin the drinking experience. When a venue has the look right you either notice because it clearly adds to the atmosphere or you don't because everything blends in beautifully. Much of this is down to personal tastes, but on the simple side, make sure you get the right glass for the job (Don't put margaritas in a

Wine Glass), and match the style to your venue. If you think it doesn't matter, you might do well to find someone passionate about "the look" and get their input.

The Volume - Much of getting the volume of your glassware correct comes down to perception. You charge based on how much alcohol is in your drinks. If your drinks are too expensive for your guests, they will likely not be your guests for so long.

Your cocktails can be made to taste correct and look good in the glassware you select.

Know your competitor's pricing and know that the gal next door might not be your competitor.

Even once you have selected the right volume glasses for your business, you need to measure a sample of each glass you select. Whether you are using free pint glasses or purchasing specialty highball glasses, trusting every glass from every company can get you into trouble. I measure one of each glass my clients stock and often find that the glasses they have are off from the quoted volume by up to 4 ounces. The best way to measure the volume of a glass is with a scale. The process is simple.

Place the glass on the scale and "zero" the scale (the scale should read 0g with the glass on it)

Fill the glass to the top with room temperature water.

1 gram of water = 1 milliliter of water, so all you have to do at the end is convert from milliliters to Ounces with any number of free apps.

Nothing Works Forever

"Never is too much of a word. Nothing lasts forever."
– Martin Van Creveld

For all of the systems and processes we discuss in this book, there is no important process more commonly overlooked than the review. We live in a world where "Set it and forget it" is more the norm than it should be. It is rare that something we build today will still apply to our business in its exact state a year or two from now.

For every process a bar needs to run well, that system deserves regular review and, when it makes sense, revamping. As the businesses we work in grow and evolve so must the way we run them. Constantly looking for ways to improve ensures we stay relevant and prosperous in a challenging industry.

A few of the major processes to review are:

- **Menus:** Review what is and what is not selling well. Listen to your guests and adjust your menu no less than once a year. This goes for cocktail lists just as much as it does for the food you serve.

- **Training Programs:** As you learn what does and does not work behind your bar, you will need to train your staff accordingly. New cocktail menus require training on the ingredients, builds, and any new techniques needed to prep and build them. Sometimes you will even need to revamp an entire training program to match changes in staff.

- **Equipment:** Bar tools wear out and need to be replaced. New better stuff sometimes even comes on the market that might make your bar run more smoothly. The toolkits you keep for each bar station need to be reviewed much more regularly than most; monthly at the least, to ensure that your staff has every tool they need to stay successful.

- **Financial Review:** It may seem like there is one and only one best way to do this, but not everything works for every business. From your shift count out procedures to Monthly cost of goods review, to your P&L, you want to make sure that you have the right data in front of you and are taking the actions needed to both run and improve the business regularly.

- **Customer Service Process:** This is the most important of all to keep in front of due to how easy it is to lose sight of and how detrimental it can be to the business. Service creep is insidious and happens so slowly that you may not even notice you have an issue until you have a cancer in your business that you need to aggressively resolve. You need to both measure your staff's habits to make sure they are holding to whatever standard and process you have created as well as to review your training and implementation process to ensure your guests are getting the service you need to keep being successful.

Keep this in mind: Just because you created something amazing a year ago, it does not mean that thing is still being implemented properly or is still working for your business.

Service

Service is the simplest expression of Hospitality. The places I know that stand the test of time are those that completely understand this principle. Providing exceptional service and delivering on reliable differentiated experiences is what drives success in our industry. As Will Durant once said in an interpretation of Aristotle "we are what we repeatedly do. Excellence then is not an act but a habit." In the following chapters we will outline some simple steps and processes that will allow you to drive sustained excellence.

The Hostess with the Mostess

"Making a strong first impression is as important as ever, especially when meeting face to face."

-Joseph Abboud

What if I told you that you can get a customer to commit to coming back to your venue before they've ever received their appetizer, entree, or even a glass of water? Sound unlikely? Not as much as you may think. Consider this: we know people choose where they dine or enjoy a cocktail based on the experience provided to them. That experience is largely a people driven event. Here's my contention. Typically, the highest paid hourly person working a busy shift is the host/hostess, yet they are given bare minimum duties and expectations. We have a huge maximization opportunity here.

"Hello! How many? High top or booth? Your server will be right with you."

Most might say that sounds perfect. Contrast that with this experience...

"Hi, welcome to Ned's Tavern! Have you been here before?

No? - Welcome, we're so glad you chose to try us!

or

Yes? - Thanks so much for coming back!

Do you have a favorite section or seating preference? John will be your server tonight. While you're waiting, here are your menus and a list of our drink specials. Tonight, we have live music beginning at 9 p.m. I'll see you again on the way out!"

It's really not much to ask for 20 seconds of meaningful dialogue and you immediately set the tone of "you are very important to us." Regulars and repeat customers choose their destinations based on how you make them feel, not necessarily how the food tastes, the beer selection, or even price. This is by no means to suggest food or price doesn't matter, of course it does, but serve an amazing meal with poor service and the result will be disastrous. Serve an average meal with amazing service and you'll get a repeat customer.

I'm focusing on the hostess position simply because it is a wildly underutilized resource in almost every venue I encounter. Most hostesses are taught simply the "what" of their job but never the "why". Why do we have a hostess? How do they set up the perfect visit? Why are they so important to the venue? Explain these things and you'll find Gen Y (WHY)'ers will respond in ways you may not have expected.

So how do we get that customer to commit to returning before the food or drink even arrives? Wow them at the door, make them feel important from the second they walk in and have your server follow up in the same vein.

- "Welcome!"
- "Have you been here before?"
- "What do you enjoy/ what have you tried?"
- "In the mood to try something different?"
- "Let me take you through our specials."
- "What questions might I answer for you?"

So the idea is to connect with customers and make them feel special; the difference is profound. See Chapters 25 and 26 **"Heads-Up"** and **"Building a Bar Community"** as well. We drive loyalty as well as increase revenue for venue and server alike. Ultimately people will say we are in the hospitality business. I think we are in the Experience Business and every interaction matters. Everyone has a role to play in creating a positive memorable experience and your host is no exception.

Heads Up

"You have to stay alert. You've got to keep raising your game."

– Larry Wilmore

A horse walks into a bar. No one notices because the bartender fastidiously focuses on cleaning glasses and prepping for the next 5 minutes.

It doesn't take a complex cocktail program for a bartender to lose sight of the most important facet of every bar and restaurant. While it has never been any different in my book, more and more managers are starting to realize again that customer service is the most important aspect of any and every bar and restaurant out there. The trap that so many bar programs fall into is allowing customer service to become a set of steps in a transactional process.

- Say Hi
- Place Menu
- Focus on stuff behind the bar
- Get order
- Make Drinks
- Clean up build station
- Focus on stuff behind the bar.

In many of the bars I spend time in; so much potential customer interaction is lost to singularly focusing on work that needs to be completed to keep things running. Of course, this work is vital to the operation of the business and even as a part of customer service, but it cannot get in the way of maximizing guest interactions. It took me months of actively practicing looking at the faces around the bar while washing glasses, building drinks, and moving from station to station before it became natural for me to keep my head up while working.

Unfortunately, there is no single list of what people should be able to do while working the crowd in every bar in the world. Your bar footprint, complexity of your cocktail list, the age of your staff (time under employment there), and so on will determine where you need to focus here. The great news is that the steps you need to take to get you moving in the right direction are few and simple; mastery is only pig-headed determination and focus away.

I highly recommend working through the following process on paper or on a great task organizational site like Asana (free and awesome). This is not something most people can do in their head.

- Identify staff who currently have their heads up the most, interacting with guests as much as possible while they work without sacrificing quality of work in the process. Add them to your team to figure out the best practice for your bar.

- Figure out which processes absolutely require focused direct attention. - There are things you need to do where your head just has to be down.

- Look hard for all steps behind the bar that you should be able to learn to a point of muscle memory. Challenge the status quo to find places where staff can work, look, and chat lightly with guests.

- Focus on shifting habits with your bartenders for one bar process at a time. I.e. you don't need to stare at your mixing glass while you stir your old fashioned.

We also go into more detail on this in Chapter 26 – **"Building a Bar Community"** be sure to check it out for some specific ways to ensure customer engagement.

Each new habit may take weeks or even months to get right with your team, but don't get discouraged. Be sure to read Chapters 2 and 3 **"Candor with Kindness"** and **"Staff MeetingsB** for communication tips. Even if you are making tiny progress each week, you are still making progress.

Building a Bar Community 26

"I got a job as soon as I graduated from school. I always wanted to bartend because I love listening to people and how miserable their lives are."
– Anthony Mackie

D o you ever wonder why some seemingly average bars just take off while other great concepts never reach their full potential? Truth is, because they're not actually average.

The old adage 'never judge a book by its cover' has never been more apropos than in the bar and restaurant business. There are a lot of determining factors to failure and success, but one consistent thread is that the failed bars never built their bar community. So, what's a bar community you ask? Imagine that bar that's reasonably busy on a typically slow night. That place you can walk into at 2 p.m. and it's full of customers. This doesn't happen by accident.

Now, if you ask the bartenders of those full places, they often can't give a prescription for how this is done, but you will find a common thread throughout each one; they've built their bar community. Let's explore what that means in real terms.

A great bar team, managers and bartenders, invest in getting to know each guest in a meaningful way. They know each client well enough that they not only connect with them on a personal level, but they begin connecting guests to other guests. In effect, they convert 'a bar' into 'my bar,' a place where people know that anytime they visit there will be people they know present, not just staff, and a reliable service experience that meets or exceeds their expectations. The best visual on this would be the old TV show Cheers where Norm walks through the door and the whole bar shouts out his name, "Norm!" No matter what Norm's experience for that day may have been up to that point it has now become a little better because of his bar community. When you think about the show's concept, it's centered around a group of people who have come to know each other via their local bar facilitated by its bartenders. Cheers became their second home.

When we have built connections that include bartender to customer, customer to customer, and concept to customer we create a holistic experience that drives not only loyal repeat business but net promoters as well, and these people become the most powerful marketing program you can ever hope to create.

Make these connections for your guests and you'll drive repeat customers into your business.

When I ask managers, "What's the most important thing we do each day?" I get a myriad of answers but the one we're looking for is, "get people to come back" and come back frequently. The more reasons we give people to return the more likely we are to win big! Here's a couple interesting statistics.

A study by Bain and Company suggests the average customer spends 67% more in months 31-36 than in the first 0-6 months so the more tenured your guest, the greater the spend.

A McKinsey study confirms that 20-50% of all purchasing decisions come by word of mouth.

So, consider carefully what you're cultivating at your bar. You can see great customer service happening from across the room. You can also see great disengagement. Be sure to move quickly when you are actively disengaged from your guests and reward your team when you see them actively engaging and creating their bar community.

Here's an awesome way to coach your team on this, we call it bartending easy as P.I.E.

- **P stands for making it personal.** People want to be greeted and we should know everybody's name. A good best practice is always use people's name on their ticket. The other thing to do is practice calling people by their name and it will eventually stick and become habit. Spend some time going through the menu, whether it's drinks or food, and invest in knowing their preferences.

- **I is for interact.** Now that we've made a strong introduction our goal is to converse with our guest. Ask how was their day, what their interests are, what's their line of work, where are they from? These are the bits of information that will allow us to make connections to other guests and build that community.

- **E is for Emotional.** Emotional connections are the most powerful. This is where we tap into how people feel. Are they having a good day or a bad day? Are they here to celebrate or even mourn? This is where bartending starts to become a little bit like psychiatry but if you make the effort you can create a friend for life. It's not as hard as it sounds; it's mainly about listening and responding accordingly. You don't need to give advice; you just need to be an active participant in your guest's experience.

These actions by your staff are easy to observe. As a manager you need to be actively observing and coach in the moment to make sure your team is executing your service strategy in a way that drives loyalty and repeat business.

The Dessert Paradox

"I am crazy for dessert. I eat everything. No one should be denied anything...just don't eat the whole thing."
– Keri Russell

A re you like most everyone out there who has dessert on the menu but you rarely ever sell it? What if I told you, you can drive dessert sales with a little psychology properly executed? Interested? Read on my friends...

- **Step One:** Most of us have been eating all our lives, hence we know how much food we require to satisfy our hunger. Nobody orders food so that at the end of their meal they still remain hungry. Hence, step one is very basic. We must introduce the idea of dessert at the outset of the visit as we do our review of the menu.

- **Step Two:** People are pack creatures, millions if not billions of years have taught us that being in a pack draws a certain level of comfort. So, now that we've planted the seed of dessert it's time to harvest. When we sell our first dessert to the table as a result of our great menu introduction, we must anchor that sale. What do I mean? Identify the most likely buyer in the group. When we sell dessert to that first person in a group of say six and no one else orders dessert what happens? Yes, pack mentality kicks in and that person will in turn cancel their order as they don't want to be the only one in the pack eating dessert.

It's at this point we must anchor that sale by immediately telling the customer we'll bring extra spoons and napkins so they can share if they desire. Now we have brought the entire pack into the experience and they know they will not be eating alone even if no one else orders.

- **Step Three:** Once people are in the pack and comfortable that they belong by way of sharing, an interesting thing happens; they want to be different. How often do you sell two chocolate lava cakes to a table? Not often, so now we want to offer our other dessert options to the balance of the table. If we are to sell a second dessert it will almost certainly not be a second order of the same item and off we go to dessert land.

In review...

- **Step one:** sell dessert at the outset of the visit.
- **Step two:** anchor the first sale.
- **Step three:** emphasize the other items to share so people can exercise their natural desire to differentiate!

Now, where's that lava cake?

Every Ounce Counts

"Practice does not make perfect. Only perfect practice makes perfect."

– Vince Lombardi

Consistency matters not just for guest experience but for margin management as well. Your cocktails are priced and designed to achieve a certain objective in both experience and cost. When we ad lib we put those outcomes at risk. We also need to be aligned on our standard pours and practicing our craft. When I read the book" Outliers" authored by Malcolm Gladwell, his studies suggest it takes ten thousand hours of practice to achieve mastery in any given field. So how much does your team practice their craft and do we think of ourselves as masters of our craft? Let's dive into this further. Here are our key points, a couple of which have their own dedicated chapters.

- Ring in all orders – See Chapter 29 - **'Ring It and Bring It'**

- Knowing how to handle draft beer issues – More detail found in Chapter 21 – **"Beer Lines"**
- Know your standard pour size; this can vary significantly.
- Be sure everyone is aligned on recipes.
- Practice makes perfect.

You may be surprised to find out how often bartenders don't know their standard pour and there is a huge financial difference between a two ounce pour and an ounce and a half pour. We want to make sure this is perfectly understood. In addition, do we pour more and charge more for a rocks pour? Is our double a true double and are we charging appropriately? All these things need to be well defined for everyone that works at your bar. This is all content that should be addressed in the training process and reviewed on a regular basis. Be sure to read Chapter 3 – **"Staff Meetings"** to review how to conduct a quality meeting.

I'm always interested in seeing how people get to their standard pour. Do they do an eight count, a six count, or do they not count at all, they just know how much goes into each cocktail (never a good answer)? Even those of you using jiggers and thinking this prevents you from having pouring issues, guess again!

As a recent example, we had a client who had 40% liquor loss in their business, yet they were jigger pouring every cocktail. There's a chasm between using jiggers and using jiggers properly. In this particular venue they simply poured into a jigger and then did it again or trail poured after the jigger was full. It wasn't until we did a training session that we learned that nobody explained to the team how to use them properly and what the exact quantity of each spirit was supposed to be for each cocktail. Now, the manager insisted that he trained the staff correctly in the first place so somewhere between being told during training and zero follow up they found themselves at a 40% loss in the business. Eventually with a lot of coaching they were able to drive their variance from 40% loss all the way down to 5% loss at the bar. Communication, verification, and follow up won the day.

It's not at all uncommon for bartenders to have a lot of inconsistency in how they prepare drinks and cocktails. There is no better example than the Bloody Mary. We've all heard, "How I make mine is…" There are a few reasons as to why this is a bad idea, atop the list is an inconsistent guest experience. A better practice is to go ahead and define the different Bloody Marys you make rather than it be totally dependent upon who's bartending on any given day. This is true for any cocktail on your menu, not just the Bloody Mary, but the BM is a great example that everyone can relate to.

The last bit here is being sure to have some version of practice set up for your bartenders. I like having a small digital scale that you can place glassware on with the pour to validate results. I prefer this over other tools on the market because it allows you to emulate an actual pour better than anything else. The main point is to make sure you have your staff practice pre-shift to ensure their pour cadence is right. If you're not practicing to create consistency, the odds of your pours being accurate are extremely low and remember, using jiggers is no guarantee; all tools must be used properly. If you get to a point where you don't think you or your team needs to practice just ask yourself if you've put in your 10,000 hours!

Ring it then Bring it

"Good habits are worth being fanatical about."

- John Irving

A great starting point for any bar manager is to ensure we ring in everything we sell. There's an all too common habit in our industry of "batching" orders in our head. How often do you see a bartender at a busy bar hovering over the POS, scratching their head and trying to recall everything a particular customer has ordered over the past couple hours?

A few negative things happen here. One is that default miss is typically in the favor of the guest, so if we're not sure if they had three or four beers our default is typically to bill for three and the house eats the error. Next, this takes us away from interacting with our guests for long periods of time which is not good for building your bar business (see Chapter 26 – **'Building a Bar Community'**) and finally, we build a bottleneck into our demand where we now potentially have a backlog of demand at our bar.

A good bell weather for if this is if you have high losses in bottled beer. This is also why we advocate for external inventory management. Bottle beer loss should be in the range of 0-1%. If you're experiencing high degrees of bottle beer loss, this could be where your problem lives. Next, this is easily observed. If you're paying attention you can see bartenders batching orders very plainly; that's when we coach in the moment. Let's review this a little deeper.

Be sure to coach in the moment but also be careful not to coach in front of guests. Those experiences can be uncomfortable and that's not the idea. Guests should never be exposed to coaching in the business. The Do's and Don'ts are:

Don'ts:
- Batch orders in your mind (trying to memorize guests orders)
- Lose time hovering over the POS trying to use recall. This then becomes both inaccurate and inefficient.

Do's:
- Ring in every transaction as they occur.
- Frees you up to interact with guests.
- Eliminates worrying about incorrect orders.

Remember: We target 0% bottled beer loss!

Order of Operations

"And now the sequence of events in no particular order."
– Dan Rather

"One Guinness, a Gin and Tonic, a Mojito, and two shots of Jack please". I could make that order properly in 3 different ways that would take between 2 and 5 minutes at top speed. In an industry where seconds per order can equal hundreds of thousands of dollars in profit per year, getting the build order right is important.

Getting your build order perfectly set will drive your ability to maximize your revenue per hour. Your guests will be happier when they get their drinks as quickly as possible; which I would argue is even more important than the increase in revenue.

Sadly, unlike the algebra that I know every one of you fell madly in love with in Junior High, there is no defined order of operations for building drinks. Fortunately, if you answer the following questions about your business, you can work towards guiding your staff to a process that maximizes revenue and makes your customers fall in love with your ability to serve.

The beginning: There are drinks in your business that will require more time or "special" time during their creation. There are drinks that cannot afford to sit too long or they are ruined. If you serve Guinness the right way, you are looking at nearly 2 full minutes; but the process breaks into two parts with a rest in the middle...so why would you pour a Guinness last? A Miller Lite loses its head in seconds, why would you pour a Miller Lite first? In the perfect world, you want to get your customers their drinks in the best possible condition every time; it is foolish to leave the decision of what to make to when for the time when your staff is in the weeds.

The process to figure out your process is to:

- **Start Top end:** Determine which category of drink takes the longest to serve and which take the shortest to serve.

- **Start to Get Specific:** Think about which drinks have a build time that is longer than other drinks in the same category.

- **Get special:** Determine any drinks that need to "rest" before being served or have a two- part creation process. Conversely, which drinks will lose their luster if they sit for "too Long"?

- **Pre-Plan:** Figure out which drinks can have parts of their build completed ahead of time in batches.

  o **Simplest example:** Pre-batching Simple Syrup can more than half the time it takes to make a mojito.

  o **More complex:** Are you putting .25 oz Campari, 0.5 oz sweet vermouth, and .75 oz St. Germain into your most popular cocktail? Make a batched cheater bottle of the three that your staff can pour 1.5 oz of into each cocktail.

- **Stock your wells properly:** Another name for the "Well" is the "Speed Rail". Over time, in many places, "The Well" has come to mean "Cheap". This does not have to be the case. It is true that wells tend to be stocked with the less expensive products carried in a venue; however, inexpensive does not have to equal low quality. In addition to this, you are going to want to have your top movers in your wells; which might not necessarily be your most inexpensive products. With most POS systems, it is very simple to pull your top 10 movers out. Make sure that all spirits represented in your top ten are in your speed rail; make it easy for your team to get those high-volume products over the bar as fast as possible.

One last thought: As we discussed in Chapter 23 - **'Nothing Lasts Forever'** you will need to revisit your order of operations at least once a quarter. As seasons change, so can your top 10 shift.

Timing Benchmarks 31

*"I'm such a profound believer that timing is everything; I
would tattoo that on my arm."*

– Drew Barrymore

I want you to think about your personal level of patience.
How long does it take before you notice that it has been
"too long" since your server last visited your table? For
each diner in your restaurant, there is a line that is crossed in
service that is hard to come back from. This ranges from person
to person, but the age of social media has made this time frame
shorter for most people.

Ninety seconds. That is the average time that a viewer
leaves a YouTube video. Video services like YouTube have
been training us to tune out more quickly than we did in the past
and they aren't the only format to do so. People were so strongly
tied to the quickly digestible 140 characters on twitter that the
new 280 character limit was fought and squashed the first time
it was proposed and both hated and mocked when it was finally
released.

To top this all off, the same services that make broadcasting bad experiences easier than ever are some of same exact tools that have made people less patient.

Timing is key to making sure you are controlling one of the most emotional aspects of the guest experience, and one that you have to be extremely aware of as you are managing your bar. There are key service points that need to be set and constantly measured to ensure you do not become that place where it takes "forever" to get a drink; even when forever is 90 seconds. The times below are a starting point and should not be treated as absolutes. For example, if there are 3 people sitting at a bar, a new guest should be greeted in around 5 seconds.

- Time to acknowledge guest (at each point; host stand, bar, etc…) – 5sec to 10 sec
- Time to server/bartender greet - 30 seconds or less.
- Time to water on the table - 30 seconds or less
- Time to first ordered beverage - 1 to 3 minutes
- Time to first order taken - 1 to 3 minutes (coincide with drinks dropped)
- Time for apps to come out - 7 to 10 minutes after order placed.
- Time for Mains to come out. - 15 to 20 minutes after order placed.

- Time for check delivery - 60 seconds or less after requested.

On the opposite side of the equation is the design phase of menu building. Not only do you need to take care to build a quality menu that is serviceable by your staff, you must consider how long each cocktail and dish takes to build.

This gets even more complex when you start to consider different service periods. For example, you can have a beautiful, award winning cocktail list for which each drink takes 90 to 120 seconds to build; however, when you are 3 deep at the bar, it might be prudent to place an altered menu where each cocktail takes a max of 30 seconds to build. The same can go for food; a 15-minute lunch menu can attract a business crowd with time restrictions on their lunch break.

Ultimately, getting timings right on both ends has benefits for both your guests as well as the operations of the house. Once you have determined what works for your business, continuous measurement will ensure your times are being hit...people respect what you inspect.

Service Recovery

"To give real service you must add something that can't be bought or measured with money, and that is sincerity and integrity."

- Douglas Adams

This may be the service version of hair of the dog. So many venues do not define clearly the steps to fixing a problem. There is a very specific way you should go about doing this from recognition through resolution. If you want to avoid negative reviews on social media, here's where it starts. The real beauty of fantastic recovery is that we can create a better experience for a guest than if nothing negative had happened in the first place; imagine that!

When something goes awry during a visit it gives us the opportunity to show a guest just how very important they are to us. Let's go through this in a very simple step by step way.

- **Step one: Recognize.** Through the course of interacting and heads-up bartending it should never come as a surprise when we have an issue. Whether it's a quality issue, timing issue, or service related, we should notice. Through the process of heads-up bartending and watching the room we should actually have multiple people recognize an unhappy guest. People are usually a pretty easy read in this regard.

- **Step two: Activate.** Make sure your team is empowered to fix problems. These are the same people we trust with our service promise, cash, opening the venue, inventory and more, so doesn't it make sense we can also trust them to take care of an issue? I'm always reminded of a story Sean Finter tells about having a problem with a baked potato at a fairly well-known restaurant chain. After discussing it with the server, a manager came out to check on the problem and then went about replacing the potato. Sean then quipped, "I just wanted a new potato. Does that require a manager's approval?" So, the idea is, don't kill a fly with a sledge hammer. Enable your team to fix small problems quickly and with a smile. They can and should inform you as necessary but let's not slow down the fix; let's give the right measure of response.

- **Step Three: Make the right correction.** It's not unusual to have an issue such as a poorly prepared meal that a customer sends back followed by a response of free dessert. What does a free dessert have to do with fixing the entrée issue? Where it may seem generous it actually misses the mark. If you want to fix the issue, comp the entrée and get them their meal, not a dessert they never ordered and don't want. You may come back with an offer to return and "dessert is on us" but not in lieu of fixing the problem. It would purely be additive in the hopes of showing genuine care. The fix should match the problem.

- **Step Four: Follow-up.** As a Manager this is where you want to be present. It's always good form to follow up with authenticity to ensure the problem was fully resolved by your team. Showing how much you care is what people really want to see. Most people understand mistakes happen. How much that mistake matters to you as the Manager is what will make or break their final opinion. So, Recognize, Activate, Fix the Right Problem, and Follow-Up and you just may find you have a bigger advocate than if nothing had gone wrong at all!

It's on me!

"*I really, really pride myself on being a professional and a man of keeping my word. It means a lot to me, truly.*"
– *Charlie Hunnam*

There is a common but misguided concept in our industry, - If I give away free drinks, I will get more/bigger tips; or if I pour strong drinks, I will get more/bigger tips. I thought the same thing when I first started working in restaurants. It is ingrained in the culture and we pass this idea from one to another.

I was fortunate to meet a few amazing people early in my restaurant career who taught me a different outlook; the correct understanding of the best way to make money when you are working for tips.

Ultimately, this comes down to being a professional.

- **Pros hone their skills**, fighting to be the best they can in their field. If your staff can't pour the pour size of your venue within 95% accuracy every single time, no matter the situation, they are not a pro.

- **Pros don't cheat others for their own financial gain.** Criminals do, pros don't. Once you understand that every free drink you put across the bar, whether in a single glass as an unpaid double or as a separate drink, comes from someone else's hard-earned dollar (the owner), it should be clear that giving away free drinks and over pouring intentionally is pure theft.

- **Pros dress the part.** Whether your venue has a uniform or not, take pride in your appearance. You will find out it's a very select, very small group of people who want to drop large tips to a dirty or disheveled bartender on a regular basis.

- **Pros have their shift together.** Your staff who arrives early and sets their bar up to make sure they can serve their guests as quickly as possible during their shift will likely be your top earners.

- **Pros leave their problems at home.** Harsh truth time: We all have bad days and, outside of your friends and family, no one cares. People do not go to bars to be dumped on, complained to, ignored, or otherwise treated in any way other than with great service and engagement. Leave your problems at home and find a friend to talk to about it after your shift...preferably at someone else's bar.

- **Pros don't come to work hungover.** This one is a personal pet peeve. If your hangover looks, smells, or sounds like the devil crapped you out after completing the Taco Bell 30 burrito challenge, don't be hungover for a shift. No one wants to see that and again, no one wants to hear about how tired and in pain you are because of your hangover.

To take this thought a step further, bragging about how drunk you got and how epic your hangover is stops being cool after college. No guests think you are cool for being able to polish a fifth of Jameson by yourself; they are probably wondering how best to ask if you need help.

- **Pros know how to pull the biggest tips.** The most important factor in maximizing your tips is to provide exceptional, speedy service (see Chapter 31 – **"Timing Benchmarks".)** However, there is one trick that is amazingly effective and that I would not have believed had I not seen it for myself

One of my early mentors was a man we called Irish Dave who worked with me at Slainte in Baltimore, MD. A bartender from Mumbai, India, Irish had a simple habit that made him the hands down top tip earner in our business (he pulled $200+ more than any other bartender per shift on average and he only worked lunches). All of our bartenders had a comp tab each shift; Dave was the only one who never used it. He still gave certain, very select customers free drinks; the difference is that Dave would pay for them himself. Without being gaudy, he would make sure his customers knew that it was him paying for the drinks, not the house; and they understood the significance and showed their appreciation in kind. Combined with his dedication to high professionalism, this made him a very successful earner.

The proof was clear when Barmetrix was brought into where Irish and I worked. The owner had every bartender individually audited without their knowledge multiple times; Dave was never missing a drop of liquor during his shift; Top earner, zero loss.

<u>What's going on here?</u>

"Communication leads to community, that is, to understanding, intimacy, and mutual valuing."
– Rollo May

If you're like most bars, you are always looking to increase revenue. Often, we look towards entertainment to drive additional value into the business. That may be music, poker, trivia, karaoke, or any other number of creative ideas people come up with to drive foot traffic into the bar. So often we see these investments made by ownership, yet, no communication is made by staff to entice or inform people of the many activities happening within the venue.

For example, as we mentioned in Chapter 26 - **'Building a Bar Community'** we want to get to know each guest on a personal level. In those dialogues lie the perfect opportunities to promote the many benefits of visiting your venue on other nights. We should be constantly promoting why we are the best choice for spending their dollar. All too often we see the investments made in entertainment without the subsequent effort to drive awareness to our valued guest. Maybe they'd really enjoy a night out of karaoke, live music, or trivia on another evening with you. Let's make sure they are aware.

Another thing we see a lot are posters and billboards which advertise all the events a particular venue has to offer and that's great! We encourage advertising but not in lieu of dialogue from the staff. All our social media and in-venue promotions should be viewed as additive; as covered further in Chapter 8 **"Social Media Management"**.

The perfect time to remind a guest of our many entertainment offerings is when we present the check. "We'd love to see you back for karaoke on Friday or trivia on Wednesday," etcetera.

I happened to be listening the Michael Smerconish radio program on Sirius XM 124 one day as he discussed a commencement speech he gave at Temple University. The premise of the speech was essentially "ask for the order." In effect, if you don't ask for what you want you are very likely to not receive it.

This is so very true in any sales position. Often bartenders and staff don't think of themselves as sales people, but they certainly play that role. Bartenders are selling themselves, products, and entertainment to guests every day. It may be in a more non-traditional subtle way but it's certainly selling. Our industry is always striving to drive more revenue into our venues, yet we tend to shy away from promoting our many wares in front of our captive audience.

So, be sure your bartenders and servers are well-aware of all your entertainment offerings in the same way you make sure they are aware of food and drink specials. The teams should incorporate this information into their regular dialogue throughout guest visits. Then get this information locked in as part of your regular close dialogue much the same way we may say, "Thank you and please come back and see us!" You may want to include, "We have trivia on Wednesday and live music on Fridays! I know you said you like both and there's no better place to be than here!" However you do it, just be willing to do as Michael suggests and "ask for the order!"

A Smile across the room

"Most smiles are started by another smile."
– Frank A. Clark

I have seen truly impressive training programs backed by robust manuals and fortified with beautifully produced videos. I have seen beautifully run and managed restaurants where it is clear that everything is working perfectly and others, with a nearly identical emphasis on training, where the team can't figure out why nothing ever seems to go right.

You cannot be everywhere at once. This sounds stupidly obvious, but it is a vital issue that you need to overcome when running a bar. Fortunately, the solution is simple. You don't have to be in every location in the restaurant, you just have to see them on a regular basis throughout your shift. I want you to consider that, for most processes that must work well in your business, if you cannot see it from across the room, you cannot manage it.

The simplest example of this is the ubiquitous smile.

One of your main driving goals as a restaurant operator is to make your guests happy, it's almost in the definition of what you do. But how do you know if your staff is making your guests happy from across the room? Simple - are your guests smiling?

When pointed out this way, it seems so obvious as to not be useful advice; however, in practice, it is easy to lose sight of this simple principle and not look around for smiling faces. Additionally, you can apply this to other, more practical and simple practices in the businesses.

Are the bussers clearing tables in a timely manner? - Look for any objects that the guest no longer needs on the table.

Are the servers keeping beverages properly topped off? - Look for any glasses that have 2 fingers less in the bottom of the glass.

Are your tables getting reset the moment a party leaves?

It is just as easy to overcomplicate your training program as it is to create a great one that is near impossible to manage. When considering where to focus your training (or retraining if you are struggling with a specific aspect of operations), the best rules, practices, and processes to train into your staff are those that you can see the effects of from across the room.

From the bar side, the long-distance management tool I see most consistently missed is the glass half full principle or making sure your guests' drinks are being refilled in time. I eat out a lot; it's a tough part of my job. I find it more common that I have to flag down servers and bartenders to get my drink refreshed than to have my drink refilled consistently. It is both a simple task to complete and one that, when missed, has potential to ruin an experience.

You don't have the ability to be everywhere at once or stare at glasses all day. What you can do is put it into your set rotation to observe the glasses on the table as you move from table to table or to the bar.

The best part of this one is that, when you get it right, you will see a lot more smiles from across the room.

Financials

Three years out of college, I made the transition from being a transducer design engineer to becoming the bar manager of three impeccably run venues that were right next to (and on top of) each other. I was taught how to manage six floors containing five bars with two separate kitchens in two buildings very quickly.

I was fortunate to be taught by an incredible team on how to run multiple restaurants. However, it was a few years in before I was finally taught how the P&L worked.

The financial understanding of bars and restaurants tends to be one of the most under-trained areas for bar managers. The next section is organized differently than the others. Due to the heavy nature of financials, we have separated the theory and math out in such a way that you can dig into as much detail as you want. Remember you need to be able to tie your business decisions to your financial outcomes.

The Cost Factor Part 1: Three types of COGs

"Take it from me, and start looking at these other costs from the very beginning and you'll get a clearer of just how profitable your business can run."

– Dafina Smith

Yes, there are three types of Cost of Goods (COGs). Unfortunately, the most common "cost of goods" people have shown me over the years is not actually a cost of goods figure, but I'm getting ahead of myself here. After I started working as a bar manager so many years ago, It was 6 months before my boss sat me down to explain cost of goods and how they work. I had a good teacher who had a strong understanding of the concept; however, over the last 12 years, working with hundreds of operators, I have come to realize that I was lucky and that many people out there have a very limited and often incorrect understanding of cost of goods. Finally, before I get started with the meat below, it is important that you understand that, while this is one of the more complex concepts in the book, it is also essential that you understand it if you want to run a profitable bar.

Before I get into the specifics below, you will see me switch between talking about cost and profit throughout this section. That is because cost of goods is the inverse of profit. That is; Gross Profit Percentage = 100% - COG%. For example; if my COGs are 19%, then

100% - 19% = 81% (Gross profit)

So, if my Cost of Goods are low, my profits are high.

In the simplest terms, cost of goods is how much money you spent on product compared to how much gross revenue that exact product brought in. The lower the COGs, the better.

Misconception: There is a "standard" cost of goods. I don't know where the idea of the industry standard came from, but it can be a very costly and even dangerous (for your business) concept. When looking at what your cost of goods "should" be, there are many factors that come into play that we'll get into below and in other chapters.

The Target Cost of Goods

Also commonly referred to as the Theoretical Cost of Goods, Target COG is the simplest of the three. Essentially, it is how you plan what you will make off of any one serving of one product in your business.

In short, you divide the cost of a single serving by the retail price you plan to charge for it. You can even generate an extremely generalized target for any given category or even your business by making sure all of the products in that category are close to the COG you are looking to hit.

If you think about it, you will likely realize that this target COG will lose meaning once you open your doors and your product mix, specials, happy hours, comps and so on come into play. You are never going to sell the same exact number of every item you sell at full retail price and that will drastically change your COGs. Once you are operating, target cost of Goods is best left to the single product level as you set pricing for new product you bring in and to periodically re-evaluate your pricing.

This is generally a very well understood concept in our industry that is used to set prices for products in the venue; calculating the impact of your product mix and such as mentioned above is a more complex concept that we cover in the next chapter.

The Potential Cost of Goods

The Potential Cost of Goods are the key to understanding your business. THIS is your CURRENT real target. This figure represents the very best you could have done for a particular week with the specific product mix, discounts, specials, and so on that your staff sold that week. When managers and owners ask me what their costs "should" be, this is the number that will lead to the answer.

Your potential COG is the wholesale value of what was rung into your POS divided by the total retail dollars collected for those sales. For a given week, whether that product was sold at a Discount, as a BoGo, at Happy Hour, or for full price; whatever retail dollars are collected for those sales, that will be the retail figure you use to make this calculation. I like to call this your cost of sales.

It is the best you could have possibly done for that week for what you sold at the prices you sold it for.

If this figure is higher than you need for your business to make money, you need to stop whatever you are doing and redesign your entire pricing strategy until you get to a figure that works for the business.

Once you have a strong understanding of this figure and you have optimized it for your business, the next time someone asks you what your costs "should" be, this is the figure you give them.

The Actual Cost of Goods

Many operators have an idea of what their actual cost of goods are. Quite a few even know exactly what that number is. Your actual cost of goods is what happens when you lose product. I also call this the cost of depletion as that is literally what it is. Where your potential cost of goods is calculated off of ONLY what was rung into your POS, the actual cost of goods is calculated off of everything that "left" your building. Whether an item was sold at full retail, broken, given away, paid for but never arrived, poured down the drain; if it was there at the beginning of the week and it is gone now, it goes into the actual cost of goods equation.

Here is the kicker; you have to use the exact same retail sales collected in both the Potential and Actual COG calculations. The sales are what they are. Once you add in all of the items that were depleted, but not rung in, you get a higher wholesale cost value in the equation and so the Actual Cost of Goods will almost always be higher than your potential.

Your actual cost of goods is a very broad indicator of how well you did for the week and it is a great place to start

MISCONCEPTION: Do not confuse purchases divided by sales with an actual cost of goods. I call this "Cost of Purchases and it is not an exceptionally valuable figure. If you are frustrated that your cost of goods fluctuate wildly (17% one month, 26% the next), you are likely using cost of purchases.

However, cost of goods is not good enough. Next, we will start to get into why.

The Cost Factor Part 2: Plan it!

"Read over your existing business plan like you read the menu

at your favorite restaurant."

– Darren L. Johnson

If you got your hands on this book before setting up a bar program, you have hopefully taken the first step of knowing what your COG need to be in order to make your business profitable.

What are your current cost of goods? If you don't know them, go ahead, I'll wait; this is important.

Ask yourself:

- Are they good?
- How do you know?
- Good compared to what?
- Who set that industry standard?
- Does that standard really hold up for you?

- OH, sorry, you are comparing them to last year? How do you know last year was the right benchmark for your business?

I ask these questions a lot. It is a great set of questions designed to get Bar Managers and owners to understand that for a long time, we have been duped into thinking about our COG the wrong way.

The industry standard fallacy: I've heard it from operators enough times to lose count:

> "I've been in the business for years, 20% to 24% Cost of Goods is the industry standard."

I am so very sorry; but there is no real industry standard. There are guidelines that can get you in the right ballpark, but I know guys who would burn their bar down if they saw a 22% COG and others who would throw the party of the century for numbers like that. I have seen "good" COG ranging from 12% to 30%; it all depends on the business.

The "Down from last year" circle of hell: Shortly after starting with Barmetrix a decade ago, I heard my first "We want to be 1.5 points down from last year and we will be good" line of thinking. That venue was another 4 points and $150,000 a year off from what their Actual COG should have been due to standard industry losses.

At the risk of being redundant; there is no singular industry standard. Also, setting your benchmarks by last year is the blind leading the blind unless you had a "real" number to start with; garbage in garbage out.

You can get an idea of around what your COG should be by considering your:

- Type of business (club, neighborhood bar, etc…)
- Exact geographical location
- Type of clientele (What your customers will bear)
- Cost of the products you are stocking.

but that is a more complex conversation. Ultimately, your COG have to be tied to the answer to one vital question:

What does my overall cost of goods need to be in order for MY business to make money?

Before you open your doors; before you even break ground or start to remodel the space you want to buy; before you spend a penny, you want to create a strong financial model that incorporates your actual rent/lease payments, loan payments, and all other fixed costs. If you did not do this, it is never too late to reassess and redesign your beverage program.

You also need to consider the other two prime costs: labor and energy. Finally, you need to drop in a projected, realistic revenue stream broken down between food and alcohol, based on actual figures derived from other similar businesses in the area or in similar areas. It is a lot of work and should not be rushed.

If this sounds like a P&L, that's because it is essentially what you are building; a rolling, monthly P&L for the first 3 years of the business.

This free tool from the SBA helps a lot with that and more:
https://www.sba.gov/tools/business-plan/1

Once all of that work is done, you can start to figure out what your COG needs to be in order for your bar, in your city, run with your concept, needs to hit in order to be successful. There is a little more guesswork to be done here. Take your proposed alcohol revenue and divide it by how many drinks you believe you will be selling to bring in that revenue. That will give you a rough idea of what you need to charge per drink in order to make money in your business.

Again, if you are running a bar that is struggling, you can do the same process, but with the ACTUAL numbers the business is running; it's almost cheating...

You are likely to get stuck on any one of these major points while building your initial overall target COG figure. Maybe you find that you need to sell your drinks at an average of $20 to make this work and that is just NOT going to happen in Kalamazoo. It might be time to reassess your assumptions, your figures, the deals you have for the lease, your loan, and so on. If and when you get to one of these points, you will have uncovered a huge problem that likely would have doomed your business after it was too late and that is just awesome!

Before you start, you need to understand that the outcome of this exercise might be that there is no way to make your business work with your current set of circumstances; but at least you will know.

If you are already running your business and are trying to figure out where your costs are and what they "should" be then the next chapter will take you the rest of the way there.

The Lost Shot

"I never lost money by turning a profit."

– Bernard Baruch

I n the previous chapter we discussed Potential Cost of Goods: The target of YOUR business. This defines your best-case scenario based on your sales for the week with the specific product mix, discounts, happy hour deals and so on.

We also discussed your Actual Cost of Goods: How you really performed for a given week; how your beverage program actually performed.

Now here is the most important piece of information: How you move your Actual Cost of Goods down to your Potential Cost of Goods. That is, how do you make your actual performance match your best possible performance?

The short answer is that you need to understand Variance. Variance is the difference between your Potential and actual cost of goods. This all makes sense when you break down the equations that define each of these figures.

> **Cost of Sales/Retail Sales x 100% = Potential COG**
>
> **Cost of Stock Depleted/Retail Sales x 100% = Actual COG**

The key here is to understand how Cost of Sales and Cost of Stock Depleted are related. First, what do I mean by each of these terms?

Cost of Sales is the wholesale cost of the product that you rung into your POS.

Cost of Depletion is the wholesale cost of the product that left your venue through sales AND loss.

In case it isn't obvious, the only difference between these two is the wholesale value of the variance. If you hadn't lost anything, your costs would have been as good as they possibly could have been. Unfortunately, the average bar and restaurant in America loses 20% of its stock. This is why most bars and restaurants are busy breaking even. If you are making just enough to pay yourself a decent salary, but you can't hire someone to run the business for you and still make a solid profit, you are likely in this category. Even the average well operated bars U.S. are leaving 5 and 6 figures on the table annually by not carefully controlling variance and therefore maximizing their Actual Cost of Goods.

There is a whole other side to variance that I haven't gotten into yet. So far, I have only talked to you about the wholesale losses. The real killer of variance, and why so many restaurant owners look at their bank account and wonder why they are not making all the money they thought they should, is the retail component.

Variance exists in a spectrum. On the full wholesale side is a bottle being broken but not recorded by staff, or product ordered and paid for, but not dropped off. As you move through the spectrum, you get to over-pouring, whether intentional or accidental. Over-pouring leads to product that would have eventually been paid for at full retail going into a glass for free. Of course, this is more of an opportunity loss. When you get to the full retail end of the spectrum, you are talking about full product going across the bar but not getting paid for. This can include bartenders taking multiple orders at once and forgetting a bottle of beer or two when they ring them in or, much worse, staff giving product to a guest and pocketing the cash they pay for it.

Outsourced Inventory 39

"The important thing about outsourcing is that it becomes a very powerful tool to leverage talent, improve productivity and reduce work cycles." – Azim Premji

Inventory is simply cash converted to product with the idea of making even more cash. This means we want to treat inventory with the same veracity we would treat a cash drawer or till. When we ask managers or owners about how they manage their inventory a fairly common response might be,

> "We don't have any inventory issues. We have a good system that we do ourselves."

At which point we may ask,

> *"Wonderful, can you tell me a little about what you do?"*

The response typically being…

"We count everything each week then we use those counts against a par guide that tells us what to order. If something is off, the manager will let me know."

The truth of the matter is, things are off all the time. We're dispensing liquid and whether you're free pouring or jigger pouring you will have loss issues in your business.

Recently I was sitting with the owner of one of the highest volume bars in the world. We began discussing inventory. I expected him to have a robust program in place. Interestingly it was just the opposite, just a pen and paper program that told him little more than what to order for the coming week. He had become so successful that driving to maximize profits became a lost idea because revenue was doing so well. Ironically, his very success would provide an even higher return on investment if he were to use an outsourced program like Barmetrix. By the end of our conversation, we figured that he will be looking at around a $150,000 return, every year. So, let's go through some concepts to consider when you're analyzing your own program.

- **Self-reporting:** Very few people, given the option, will report numbers on themselves that lead to their own demise. However, a talented manager doesn't fear what they know; they fear what they don't know. Good data in the hands of talent will do great things which will advances careers and create opportunities.

- **True reconciliation:** You must drill down to every drink and recipe sold, and bounce that against actual counts from previous audits plus purchases to reconcile true performance. Very few in-house solutions do this. So few, in fact, that I've never seen one. Be sure to reference Chapter 18 – **'Keys are the Key'** for more on this subject.

- **Kegs:** If you're selling kegs, it's all guess-work if you're not weighing each one and doing the same reconciliation mentioned above. Draft is an easy place to manipulate the numbers because no one can disprove how much is in a keg and nobody wants to double check.

- **Targets:** Too many bars and restaurants don't know what their ideal pour cost should be, so they live with a number that is 'good enough' based on sales and purchases. Then the team figures out how to create this number each week to make sure the boss is happy. Typically, this is simply done by purchasing fewer products in a world that is perpetually overstocked.

- **Productivity:** You put tons of hours into bad data that leads nowhere. When's the last time a bar manager could rattle off the exact loss of your top 5 items and put a plan in place to communicate and manage the loss. This should be very specific and well defined in each audit period.

- **Competency:** This isn't your core expertise (hopefully) but it is a vital component of your business. Use inventory experts so you can focus precious energy on other priorities, a great win/win.

- **Turnover:** Inventory is just another area impacted by turnover that pulls from valuable training time on the service side and other aspects of the business. Plus, when people hate doing something, they are motivated to leave. Create stability and job satisfaction by outsourcing to people who love doing that work.

- **Pushback:** If your team rejects the idea of accountability look out. Very few people want to do this, but sometimes the idea of accountability is even more frightening than counting product.

- **It's not an expense, it's an investment:** When you add it all up, it pays for itself in a big way. All the savings on loss, purchase optimization, overstock, labor savings, and reliable data pays big time ROI.

In closing, even our best accounts that run world class variance/loss figures have volatility in their business. If you can't or don't have people informing you every audit period on your biggest opportunities, you don't have a functional inventory program. The average bar runs 20% loss, world class operators run at less than 3%. An interesting statistic of our own, we've never seen a venue fail financially that ran its inventory at a world class level!

Reconcile Your Drawers

"Sometimes I am two people. Johnny is the nice one and Cash causes all the trouble."

– Johnny Cash

Every time I walk into a business and find out that a manager is not reconciling the bar tills every night, I am shocked. For a long time I thought reconciling drawers was a 100% standard practice in every bar and restaurant. There are a few reasons this is important but mostly, this is the first step in making sure that what was rung into your POS actually hits your bank account. If you are not performing this necessary task, your chances of losing cash in between terminal transactions and your cash being deposited in the bank are pretty high.

The purpose here is to protect the revenue and profits of the bar. The cash in the drawers at the end of the night has gone through a bit of a journey with many steps. It is one of the most important daily tasks you will take on and you want to take your time to focus on it in a quiet and controlled environment. Most likely you will have people yelling in your ear with music blasting in the background.

The process is simple and there are many reconciliation sheets you can find on the internet; however, it does take time.

The Benefits are:

- Reduces possibilities for staff to skim the till.
- Creates paper trail between transactions and actual deposit.
- Reduces chances of someone taking cash before deposits are made.

To do a basic reconciliation, you need the following:

- Starting Bank separated into bill types written down on a slip of paper in the drawer. The amount on the slip needs to have been verified and signed off on by the bartender who was given the drawer at the beginning of their shift.
- POS terminal sales print out; which will have
    - Cash sales (adding more cash to the drawer)
    - Credit card tips (potentially removing cash from the drawer)
- Any cash out slips - For example, if you needed to grab cash to go buy some mint for a rush on Mojitos.
- Any cash in slips - If a drawer runs out of cash

- Ending Cash in the Till separated into bill types.

The process should be separated into two parts; follow the age old adage: <u>The person handling the incoming cash should not be the same as the person handling the cash going out.</u>

- The Manager reconciles the math from the beginning till and cash out report.

- The Bartender or Server counts out the ending cash; which is then verified by the manager.

The total reported by the bartender should be exactly the amount calculated by the manager including their credit card tips. There are some people who like to have their staff pull their credit card tips as they go, but this can create so many more issues if the bartender makes a mistake in the process. You will need to figure out what your tolerance is for overages and shortages, however, $10 or less per till is a good rule of thumb.

One final thought I have is this: Your staff should never put their cash tips into your till. If you allow them to put what is essentially their own money into the drawer, then you cannot reliably determine what is theirs and what is yours.

In the age of more transactions being through credit cards, many employers are not able to pay out credit card tips during or after a shift. Instead, these tips are being included in staff payroll checks.

The P&L

"The Profit and Loss Statement tells you a lot about how your business is doing. It can also help you to determine ways that you can go about saving money so you can bring more money home!"

– Darren L. Johnson

We felt it would be apt to start our book with leadership and accountability concepts and close it with a chapter on the P&L. Everything we've discussed since chapter one leads us here. Your profit and loss statement is the financial culmination of all your hard work. Now, what we're not going to do is be prescriptive about how to read a P&L. Why? Because all P&L's are slightly nuanced and what we may teach you may not be how your owner(s) or accountant has set up your business. The point of this chapter is about access and action. As the bar manager, you need to be able to see the financial outcomes of your work. Now, we're aware of many scenarios where the bar manager has no idea what a P&L even is, let alone how to read it. So, here's your mission if you choose to accept it:

- **First: Gain access to the P&L.** If your owner(s) are reluctant to give you access, you need to convince them to grant you access to the areas in which you are directly responsible, e.g., payroll, purchases, sales, and basically all your operating cost and sales. Your P&L should also include financial targets so if you don't have access to all the line items you at least need access to the operating lines so you can see how your operating decisions are impacting the business.

- **Next: Learn how to manage up.** Managing up is simply how do you handle the boss. If you don't have access to your P&L data, you need to convince your boss to make it available. Explain to them, "Look, I've been reading this amazing book and they say I have to attach my business decisions to our financial outcomes." That should get their attention, but seriously, avoid accepting "no" for an answer. If they are hesitant to show you how much the business does or does not make, just ask for the operating lines. Your accountant or owner can create different versions of the full P&L if necessary.

- **Finally: Treat your financial data with care,** that is to say, we don't broadcast all aspects of the financial side of the business to the staff. We have a responsibility to handle our knowledge with care. What we do is set very specific business objectives based on the financials and communicate that to the team.

Example: *Team, sales are down 5% YOY (year over year) so we're going to launch some new specials and add a couple events to close the gap etc. When we close the gap we will celebrate by ... Each Monday we will cover our progress after the P&L comes out until further notice.*

This is just one example of many ways we can distill P&L data down to digestible and actionable information for your team. I do suggest you keep it tight and succinct; you can quickly confuse your team if you get the messaging wrong or if it's convoluted. Keep it tight and as it relates to communicating financials to your team. Less is more.

- **One Last Thought: This is a critical piece of your personal development.** Whether you aspire to own your own bar or not, understanding where the money goes and how it impacts business decisions is invaluable. Over the years I've seen managers make massive transformations in opinions and behaviors once they understood the financials of the business. So often owners and managers only prescribe what they want done in the business instead of why they need it done. In order to maximize success, someone must connect the dots for the people being asked to execute. Think of all the times you've heard, "Why are we doing this?" or "This is so stupid, what are they thinking?" Most likely these are actions based on financial outcomes that haven't been explained thoroughly to staff so they are confused and not on board.

Friends, until you're engaged in the P&L you're simply 'playing' business. You must understand how your business decisions impact financial outcomes. So, go talk to the boss and get access to the books.

Good luck!

Conclusion

About 8 months before we finally published, Dave Nitzel called me up and asked if I wanted to write a book with him. This would be a twelve-page "tips for our clients" freebie to give to our clients and maybe use as a marketing tool. I loved the idea, I was all in. One week later, we had 41 chapter ideas. We reviewed, conversed, we deliberated!

What the hell do we do with all this?!

A few days later, I called Dave and I said...

"Dave! You have no idea how important this book is going to be!!!!"

I was recalling my first days as a bar manager when my boss said, almost verbatim...

"Triple D… most of our industry lives by trial by fire. You have to live this industry to learn it from day one."

I finished my conversation with Dave by choosing my words carefully. I said:

"Dave, let's talk about how much trial by fire sucks."

There is a need defined by a group of people who are grossly underrepresented and often undervalued. The bar manager gets so little support and we are hoping that we gave you a formula that can help whether it's your first day on the job or you are a 20-year vet.

At some point, about halfway through writing this book, this conversation transitioned to a need that didn't fit anywhere in the framework we created. I thought about leaving this out as it feels preachy, but I have lost too many friends this way and ran with it.

Alcoholism and hard drug abuse are overrepresented in our industry to a point where we are always recognized for multiple achievements that we really don't want to be part of. Compounding the issue is that so many people seem to think this is "just how things are." I get it to a point; we work so hard every day, running our shifts, putting out fires, and keeping things from falling apart that we need and deserve to unwind; hell, I fell into the same trap for a time. The problem comes in when getting truly drunk multiple times a week becomes the normal way to let off steam after a tough shift. Outside of college, I have never heard an industry normalize excessive drinking like ours does.

Lately, the talk about mental health, wellness, and responsible living going on in our industry has been inching in the right direction and makes me so happy. I wish it had been going on for longer, but I'll take it and run; I don't want this conversation to stop now.

Three beloved people died in one week in my city recently; one was a personal friend of mine. If you are reading this book, it is likely that you either know someone in the industry who has died because of drugs and alcohol, have an idea who is next, or both. The saddest reality of the epidemic we are facing is this; everyone knows that if you are in the industry long enough, it is only a matter of time before someone you know personally will die from drug or alcohol abuse.

In the precious days after my friend died, I read a tweet that threw a lot of "too soon" anger replies. To me, this was more a case of "too late". Paraphrased, he said: We all know someone who is likely to die in the next few years and we all just laugh along as they commit slow suicide. This sad and dark statement is almost exactly what I see when I look back at the last few years leading up to the death by drugs and alcohol of someone in our industry. I decided to stop being sad about it and started up a non-profit called Restaurant Recovery with a few friends.

Ultimately, Knowledge is power, so here are some things I have learned since launching Restaurant Recovery (www.restaurantrecovery.com).

- Our Industry has the highest rate of illicit drug use
- Our Industry has the highest rate of substance use disorder.
- We have the 3rd highest rate of heavy alcohol use
- Alcohol can kill you in a night or over time all on its own, but cocaine is even better at it….
- You risk of stroke goes up by 700% for the 24 hours after you use cocaine (even your first time and casually in small amounts)
- Your risk of heart attack goes up by 300% for the 24 hours after you use cocaine (even your first time and casually in small amounts).

- Cocaine will eventually cause irreversible damage to your heart (enlargement and hardening) and the rest of your cardiovascular system.

So; I am going to plead here for a second.... If someone you care about is obviously at risk, speak up. These people are committing slow suicide; you will regret it if you just laugh along with it until they're dead.

When I started working in a bar in Baltimore, I also started drinking more heavily than I ever did in my life. It was normal to get off work at 3:00am and then party through until noon the next day. It took me a bit, but I figured it out for myself and slowed down; many of my industry friends needed someone else to speak up for them. I was lucky to be able to see that my personal and professional lives were not as separate as I thought; they are more connected than they seem at times. I spoke with Dave Nitzel about this ending, and once again, we realized that we are of the same mind. We believe you can be professionally successful, have fun, and stay physically and emotionally healthy all at the same time. That's our goal in writing this book, to provide you with at least some of that roadmap. I hope you enjoy reading it as much as we enjoyed writing it.

All of this is why we have decided to donate a portion of all proceeds to Restaurant Recovery. We believe in our industry and we believe in helping however we can.

Appendix 1: They always go Bad

I know this will shock some, but those beautiful spirits, wines, and beers you stocked your bar with don't last forever. They have both an unopened and an opened shelf life.

There is a bit of slop in the numbers below and every spirit acts differently once opened; however, the closer you get to the top end of the "spoilage range" the more likely you are to have something that does not taste the way it should. Additionally, you can drink most alcohol well past the spoilage dates listed; They aren't going to kill you, but the tastes are going to change. The more discerning your guests, the more important it is to get through your opened bottles quickly.

For all of the categories below, the time they last assumes you are storing them properly. You can Google any category below for more detail, however, the reason they spoil will give you a good idea as to what "proper" is for each.

For any and all wines and spirits, once opened, the less there is in the bottle the faster it will "go bad". The short reason is that the lower the level of liquid there is, the more gas there is for that liquid to react with and oxidize.

Some idiosyncrasies about spoilage:

- **Wine:** Oxygen is the worst for all wine; once opened, a bottle does not last long. However, wine also does not like extreme temperatures; 45 to 65 degrees is best to store.

- **Beer:** Light is the most damaging environmental factor for unopened beer. Other than that, opening a beer is the worst thing thing you can do to it.

- **Base Spirits:** These do not technically go bad. All times listed below refer to the fact that the flavors will change. So, your application of this information will depend on how much you, and your guests, care. People who care will tell you that you have 30 days to 6 months (MAX!!) before any quality product will start significantly changing once having been opened. Unopened, you have between 10 and 40 years; blink and it's gone.

- **Liqueurs/Cordials:** Overall, the note above about base spirits applies for MOST cordials. However, the more sugar, the shorter the life; the more alcohol, the longer the life. Because of this, the life of an opened cordial can vary greatly. Malibu (yes...it is closer to a liqueur than a rum) lasts about 3 months while Grand Marnier will last closer to 6.

Category	Unopened Life	Opened Life	Opened Storage
Beer	6 mo - 2 years (refrigerated)	About an Hour	In a Fridge
Sparkling Wine	3 to 5 years	1-3 Days	In a Fridge
White/Rose Wine	1 to 2 years	3 to 7 Days (drier=longer)	In a Fridge
Red Wine	2 to 3 years	3 to 5 Days	In a Fridge (when not in service)
Cellared Fine Wine	Decades in Cellar	NO!	NONONONONO!!!
Vermouth (ALL!)	1 year	3 months	In a Fridge
Fortified Wine	10 to 20 years	30 days	Away From Direct Sunlight and high heat
Liqueurs/Cordials (Low Alcohol)	10 to 20 years	30 days to 3 months (see above)	Away From Direct Sunlight and high heat

Liqueurs/Cordials (High Alcohol)	10 to 20 years	3 to 6 months	Away From Direct Sunlight and high heat
Rum	10 to 20 years	(Flavor profiles start changing around 30 days) 3mo - 1 year	Away From Direct Sunlight and high heat
Gin	10 to 20 years	(Flavor profiles start changing around 30 days) 3mo - 1 year	Away From Direct Sunlight and high heat
Tequila/Mezcal	10 to 20 years	(Flavor profiles start changing around 30 days) 3mo - 1 year	Away From Direct Sunlight and high heat
Whiskey	10 to 20 years	(Flavor profiles start changing around 30 days) 3mo - 1 year	Away From Direct Sunlight and high heat
Vodka	10 to 20 years	(Flavor profiles start changing around 30 days) 6mo - 1 year	Away From Direct Sunlight and high heat
Flavored Base Spirits	10 to 20 years	3 to 6 months	Away From Direct Sunlight and high heat

vii - Appendix 2: How many fit?

A series of simple charts showing how many shots, pints, glasses, etc… are in each of the standard containers.

Draft Beer:

	Kegs	1/2 bbl	50L	30L	1/4 bbl	1/6 bbl
How Many In It?	Ounces	1984	1690	1015	992	661
	16oz	124.0	105.6	63.4	62.0	41.3
	14oz	141.7	120.7	72.5	70.9	47.2
	12oz	165.3	140.8	84.6	82.7	55.1
	10oz	198.4	169.0	101.5	99.2	66.1

Hard Spirits:

	Bottles	750ml	1000ml	1750ml
How Many In It?	1oz shots	25.4	33.8	59.2
	1.25oz shots	20.3	27.1	47.3
	1.5oz shots	16.9	22.5	39.5
	2oz shots	12.7	16.9	29.6

Glasses of wine: (sparkling included)

	Bottles	750ml	1500ml	1750ml
How Many In It?	3oz glass	8.5	16.9	19.7
	4oz glass	6.3	12.7	14.8
	5oz glass	5.1	10.1	11.8
	6oz glass	4.2	8.5	9.9
	9oz glass	2.8	5.6	6.6

viii. - Acknowledgements:

We'd like to acknowledge some very special people without whom this book would have never been written. First up – Dave N.

First, I'd like to thank my parents who taught me what it means to answer the bell every day and work hard. Next, my wife Jeni who has hung in there through good times and bad and doubled as my editor, which was an unfairly difficult job! My children, Alex, who helped me launch the business, and Zach, Olivia and Sophia who have all done their part through audits, mystery shops, and marketing support. I'd like to recognize all of my wonderful employees who have helped make this possible: John Huckeba, Chris Beblo, Matthew Jackson, Rod Williams, Stephen Petitjean, Aaron LeMire and Brandon Sanchez. A special thank you to all my clients who have opened their doors to us and have trusted us in their business over the years. You guys inspire me every single day. I'd also like to thank a special guy named Mike Mundy who we call our personal bartender, which of course is not exactly true but he's put up with my wife and I for over 10 years and that's deserves some recognition! A special thanks to my brother Ryan Nitzel, who helped us think through some different concepts with the book. A thank you to Bradley Mickelson for the photo editing. Anytime someone can make us look just a little better than reality it's a huge bonus! I'd also like to recognize Russell Cowell for developing our website and Michael Midlane for building the Restaurant Recovery site for us.

Now…Dave D.'s turn…

Of course I have to start with Mom. Cynthia Bibik, who played both roles as both my father and mother I was growing up was an amazing mother (I LOVE YOU MOM!). I recently played single parent for 3 weeks, taking care of a single 7-year-old by myself. By day 3, I understood how amazing single parents are and what my mother accomplished over my first 18 years. An easy next on my list is my beautiful wife Damelis and my little girl; their patience with my long hours burying my head in a computer to write this thing did not go unnoticed. Furthermore, my wife is my inspiration and driving force; she is why I struck out to start a business and without that…no book! Next on the list, my amazing siblings. My brother Shawn, the most loyal man I know, who has given me enough legal advice as to bankrupt me were I to pay for it full price. My sister Heidi who has taught me more about writing than I think she realizes. Finally, my other brother, Armond who I am pretty sure believes in me more than anyone who knows me, including myself. I also want to thank the man who started my hospitality career; Patrick Russell, owner of Woody's, Slainte, and Koopers in Baltimore (GO EAT THERE!). Patrick was my first mentor in the industry and instilled the foundation of knowledge and love I have for the industry.

What can I say about Ray Walsh that has not already been said about Ireland? I have never collaborated with anyone as artistically as I have with Ray; I see him as my first true colleague. Of course, the other half of the dynamic duo; Sean

Finter. Sean is the other half of the reason I wrote this book. The how and why is not clear (Sean is a beautiful enigma), but I know I would not have done this had I not met him. I am the professional I am because of the time Sean invested mentoring me.

And from both Dave's

First, a nod to all of our Barmetrix colleagues out there who, in hundreds of ways small and large, helped guide and educate us in the ways of hospitality! We would not be here without you all! To Angus Winchester – the first to read and share his appreciation of our labor of love. Of course, thank you everyone who has taken the time to write kind words about what we have put to page; you have done more for us than we could accomplish on our own. Once again a huge thank you to Sean Finter and Ray Walsh; we would not have made it here without you both. Another huge thank you goes out to Dave Nanni who has selflessly gone to bat for us more than once.

Thank You for Reading!

Visit us at www.thebarshift.com for more content.

Made in United States
Orlando, FL
20 July 2023